INTRODUCTION TO
APPLIED CREATIVE THINKING:

TAKING CONTROL OF YOUR FUTURE

RUSSELL CARPENTER
CHARLIE SWEET
HAL BLYTHE

NEW FORUMS

NEW FORUMS PRESS INC.

Published in the United States of America
by New Forums Press, Inc.1018 S. Lewis St.
Stillwater, OK 74074
www.newforums.com

Copyright © 2012 by New Forums Press, Inc.

All rights reserved. No part of this publication may be reproduced or transmitted in any form or by any means, electronic or mechanical, including photocopy, or any information storage or retrieval system, without permission in writing from the publisher.

Library of Congress Cataloging-in-Publication Data Pending

This book may be ordered in bulk quantities at discount from New Forums Press, Inc., P.O. Box 876, Stillwater, OK 74076 [Federal I.D. No. 73 1123239]. Printed in the United States of America.

ISBN 10: 1-58107-225-2

ISBN 13: 978-1-581072-25-9

Table of Contents

Foreword .... *v*
Preface: Developing a Creative Thinking Literacy .... *vii*
Acknowledgements .... *ix*
Introduction .... *xi*
I. What Is Applied Creative Thinking? 1
II. Rationale: The Critical Importance of Applied
    Creative Thinking 7
III. The Great Debate: Can Creative Thinking
    Be Taught? 13
IV. Myths of Creative Thinking 17
V. Enemies of Creative Thinking 21
VI. Basic Creative Strategies: Shifting Perception 25
VII. Basic Creative Strategies: Piggybacking 31
VIII. Basic Creative Strategies: Brainstorming 35
IX. Basic Creative Strategies: Glimmer-Catching 41
X. Basic Creative Strategies: Collaborating 45
XI. Basic Creative Strategies: Going with the Flow 51
XII. Basic Creative Strategies: Playing 55
XIII. Basic Creative Strategies: Recognizing Pattern 61
XIV. Basic Creative Strategies: Using Metaphor 65
XV. The Creative Thinking Environment 69
XVI. Assessing Creativity from Many Angles 75
XVII. Synthesizing: Putting It All Together 81
XIII. Academizing Creative Thinking:
    The Creative Campus Movement 89
XIX. Domain-Specific Creative Thinking 95
XX. Creative Thinking and the Digital Media 103
XXI. The Creative Class: Creative Thinking
    in a Creative Environment 109
Afterword 115
Appendixes 117
    A. Creativity Articles for Further Reading 117
    B. Definitions of Creativity 123
    C. Further Exercises 131
About the Authors 135

Foreword

"I define creativity as the process of having original ideas that have value." –Sir Ken Robinson

I heard Sir Ken Robinson say those words at a general session of the Southern Association of Colleges and Schools Commission on Colleges Annual Meeting held in Orlando in December, 2011. His presentation was entertaining, informative, and fortuitous because it came only a few weeks after Hal Blythe, Rusty Carpenter, and Charlie Sweet had asked me to write a foreword for *Introduction to Applied Creative Thinking*. Imagine my pleasure when I saw that these three valued members of the Eastern Kentucky University family concluded that creativity has two outstanding traits: Novelty and Utility. Same point, fewer words; that is creativity.

I am proud to be the president of a University that values creativity. In fact, we articulate our three-fold mission as student success, regional stewardship, and making of our students informed critical and creative thinkers who can communicate. This book articulates the thoughts of three campus leaders around faculty development, especially as it applies to the teaching of creative thinking, on our campus. I should be loath to try to add to anything they have set forth, but I am going to try nonetheless.

You will find me in agreement with all they set forth in this book. However, I would like to posit the following:

- I truly believe human beings, by nature, are creative. How could anyone who has ever watched a child at play doubt it? The imagination of a child rapt in an adventure with his or her toys is, by my way of thinking, the epitome of creativity. It is outside the bounds of any box and unfettered by reality. Original ideas abound in the mind of a playing child and the value is in the utility of physical and mental development; not to mention the recreational value.

- Part of our responsibility as educators is to rekindle the innate creativity that exists within our students. That includes the important task of helping them give their creativity a focus. This could be in art, literature, or the more mundane but critical application of creative processes to solve real-world problems.

- I am convinced critical thinking is an essential component of applied creative thinking. The ability to assimilate and process information, to consider and evaluate alternatives, and to question and challenge the *status quo* or conventional wisdom are all requisite to developing an original idea that has value.

I have noted the focus of Eastern Kentucky University in making our students informed critical and creative thinkers who can communicate. One of my valued mentors, the seventh president of EKU, the late Dr. J. C. Powell, told me and others that the development of those attributes are what separates a true higher educational experience from advanced vocational/technical education. They are also requisites for leadership.

Thomas L. Friedman and Michael Mandlebaum in *That Used to be Us: How America Fell Behind in the World It Invented and How We Can Come Back* place a high value on applied creativity and exhort those of us in education to foster "Yes, and," thinking. That inspires creativity that is killed by "Yeah, but." They also quote Dov Seidman of LRN, who said:

> You cannot command collaboration and creativity. You have to inspire and create a context and an environment and a culture where it can happen—and where people [who feel] united by a shared vision will then work collectively and collaboratively to make it happen. (150)

It is my hope that we are building such an environment and culture at Eastern Kentucky University. I am proud of the work Hal, Rusty, and Charlie have put into our efforts to that end and very pleased that this book will be a creative work of value and benefit others who pursue common goals of inspiring a creative campus.

Dr. Doug Whitlock, President
Eastern Kentucky University

Preface: Developing a Creative Thinking Literacy

In October 2010, Eastern Kentucky University dedicated the innovative Noel Studio for Academic Creativity in the heart of the Crabbe Library at the center of campus. This space opened with ambitious plans of infusing creative thinking across disciplines. The dream? Create a central space on campus where students could refine communication products and practices through creative thinking. In the Noel Studio, students craft projects and information through a process of invention that draws from spaces designed to inspire students. Likewise, the Noel Studio has served as a catalyst for new programs and initiatives that infuse applications of creative thinking at EKU and in the region.

The Minor in Applied Creative Thinking is a primary example of the Noel Studio's influence on creative thinking at EKU. It is the result of over a year of planning and serves as an academic extension of the space's service, mission, and goals. The Minor in Applied Creative Thinking integrates concepts developed and honed through the Noel Studio's Happenings—informal events that promote effective communication design through creative thinking—with the campus community. Moreover, it responds to the need to develop innovative creative thinkers prepared to take on a variety of leadership roles. The minor makes creative thinking sustainable on campus, a logical and compelling next step after the Noel Studio's development.

The Noel's Studio's 10,000-square-foot space at the center of EKU's campus serves as a hub for creative energy. The program, and this book, serve as evidence that the creative campus concept has gained momentum. This book, in particular, assembles concepts explored during the first years of the Noel Studio's operation. It also attempts to energize conversations occurring about creative thinking on our own campus and far beyond. These essays are drawn from Happenings that have occurred within the Noel Studio's space in addition to collaborative efforts and conversations linking key stakeholders from across campus.

The authors bring a passion for applications of creative thinking and the collective momentum gained from the Noel Studio. In the first two chapters, we offer a definition and rationale for applied creative thinking. We then acknowledge the great debate taking place regarding the teaching of creative thinking. Chapter five discusses the myths of creative thinking. We also take on the enemies of creative thinking in hopes that our readers will also confront these inhibitors head on. We then discuss the basic creative strategies, including shifting perception, piggybacking, brainstorming, glimmer-catching, collaborating, going with the flow, playing, recognizing pattern, and using metaphor. Foregrounding space design strategies learned in the Noel Studio, we explore the creative thinking environment. We then overview creative thinking assessment as we move toward approaches for synthesis or putting it all together. As EKU's creative campus has developed, we have gathered strategies employed for academizing creative thinking through the creative campus movement. The chapter on domain-specific creative thinking pulls together our research toward the minor, looking to the disciplines for applications of creative work. We then explore creative thinking and digital media. Finally, Allison Boyd, an EKU student, offers the perspective of the creative student.

Building on the hundreds of Happenings and other events that inspire creative thinking on campus that have developed over the first years of the Noel Studio's operation, we bring together these concepts in one place. We understand that the concepts offered in this book are not the end of the conversation. With great enthusiasm for the ideas offered in this book, and the partnerships inspired at EKU, we expect further conversations and activities to emerge that highlight the power of creative thinking.

As conversations develop, so will our understanding for the ways that we internalize, read, and enhance creative thinking initiatives and programs. This book offers an early look at an emerging creative thinking literacy; that is, our approach to read and write about creative thinking. We expect this creative thinking literacy to inform and transform the campuses where we teach, learn, and grow. A literacy around creative thinking further integrates these concepts for the lifelong development of skills that help students to realize their potential and make them competitive in a variety of academic and business environments. This book represents a move toward a creative thinking literacy.

Acknowledgements

We would be remiss if we didn't offer a special tip of our collective hats to three individuals whose work greatly enhanced this text. Shawn Apostel in the Noel Studio demonstrated his unique brand of creativity by bringing our chapters to life through his engaging images. Furthermore, his cover art sets the tone for the creative thinking this book inspires. Allison Boyd not only wrote us an excellent chapter on a subject that vitally concerns her, the creative class, but also performed exhausting and exhaustive research. We are also indebted to Allison for her editorial work, especially during the final month's of the book's preparation—quite an accomplishment for this promising graduate student.

And, most importantly, we need to thank the author of our Foreword, Dr. Doug Whitlock, the President of Eastern Kentucky University. We asked him to write a few words as he has been instrumental in leading our University into the Creative Campus movement. He has created the perfect environment for us to write this text and constantly offered support.

We would also like to acknowledge Sara Zeigler, Dean of University Programs at EKU, for her unwavering support of the Minor in Applied Creative Thinking and the many creative efforts it took to write this book. Furthermore, we would like to thank Betina Gardner, Interim Dean of Libraries at EKU, for her support of the many creative happenings that have taken place in the Noel Studio for Academic Creativity during the time this book was written.

We acknowledge the many creative students at EKU from across campus but especially those whose work has inspired us in the Noel Studio. We're constantly inspired by the creativity of our students.

Introduction

Have you ever found yourself disappointed with a movie and said to a friend, "Even I could have written a better ending than that?"

Ever been stumped on a test, skipped that question, and come back later with the answer?

Ever done a group project wherein you couldn't get started until somebody else threw out an idea and you discovered you had something to build on?

How about repainting your room on a whim or putting together one of those pre-fabricated pieces of furniture without following directions?

Or better yet, suddenly had an "A ha!" moment where you figured out your own Pythagorean Theorem or Archimedes Principle?

Most likely, in all these instances you were applying creativity to a particular area of your life in order to solve a problem. Sometimes you were probably conscious of using creativity, and other times creativity just seemed to happen.

The point is that creativity is an important part of our lives, and learning to apply it helps us lead more satisfying lives. Contrary to popular opinion, everybody possesses it, but not everyone is in touch with it, understands it, or knows how to access it to solve daily problems.

Yes, as with the first example, creativity is something artists and writers employ, but they aren't the only users. They do, however, tend to be more in tune with their creativity, perhaps from relying on it more than most people do. Could just anyone write a better ending to a movie? In part that depends on the movie and the writer. Ernest Hemingway reportedly once told an aspiring author that he had to write a million words before he could become a writer.

Papa's point crosses over many areas of life and intellectual disciplines. You get better applying creativity the more practice you have doing it.

Admittedly, some people are more in touch with creativity than others, but we emphasize: creativity is a set of learnable skills.

Our second example of stepping away for a while from a problem and coming back later illustrates one of those skills. When you distance your conscious mind from a problem, you sometimes create what's called **perception shift**. Your subconscious mind continues to study the problem, aided by your distance in time, space, and concentration upon it. By seeing the problem from different or multiple perspectives, you can often get a true grasp on the solution.

For instance, maybe you're doing a crossword puzzle with the clue "low sound" and you fixate on a whisper, a "Psst." But that word won't fit, so you go get something to eat, and when you come back, you suddenly recall an old hymn where "The cattle are lowing." Eureka! A low sound is simply (and here you smack yourself) a MOO. The time and space between the kitchen table and the refrigerator have created a perception shift that helped you find an alternate answer.

Once you understand skills such as perception shift are a subset of creativity, you realize that just being aware of these skills and their usage can help you solve daily problems.

And that in a nutshell is why we wrote this book. But there are other reasons.

So much of your education has focused on **convergent thinking**—i.e., finding the right answer to the problem. Because of the current mania for testing, you were no doubt given various kinds of tests throughout your K-12 advancement. Some states even require tests to get out of high school. How often did your K-12 years focus on questions such as:

1. In what year did Columbus sail the ocean blue (bonus points for naming his three ships)?

2. What do we call the theorem that states the square of the hypotenuse of a right triangle is equal to the sum of the squares of the other two sides (we've already answered this one earlier)?

3. Who wrote *For Whom the Bell Tolls* (likewise, our intro provides a clue)?

But as you get older, you have probably come to realize that the world can't always be seen in black and white terms, that sometimes questions have no one answer, or that solutions and viewpoints can be ambiguous. For instance, the correct answer on a test for #3 is probably listed as Ernest Hemingway, but Papa actually borrowed the title from a prose-poem by John Donne called "Meditation 17." That, however, probably wouldn't be a given solution, and you, though you studied it in English class, couldn't write it in.

In other words, K-12 education in its teach-for-the-test mode focuses on convergent thinking, but another type of thinking also exists. **Divergent thinking** is a process wherein many ideas are generated in order to arrive at a solution. This type of thinking commonly occurs in environments where ideas flow freely and spontaneous, rapid-fire thinking is encouraged. Yes, sometimes one of these ideas is best for a circumstance, but it may or may not provide the "correct" answer.

When you're generating ideas, it's difficult to tell which ones have the most potential to stick. You wouldn't want to prematurely eliminate an idea before its time. You might find that one of two ideas could be combined to form a more powerful one. In divergent thinking, you'll explore many possible ideas in a short time. Most importantly, the goal is to generate them quickly.

Therefore, this book also serves as an antidote to your K-12 thinking by teaching you these divergent thinking skills.

And why is it important you also learn these skills? It is estimated that in your lifetime you will hold six to seven different jobs, and some of these jobs do not yet exist. How can college train you for unborn professions? A focus on creativity teaches you skills to adapt to the new, and more than that, to use those very skills to fabricate and shape the future.

In 2010 IBM sent out a survey to over a thousand CEOs of some of our country's largest corporations and asked what skills were considered paramount for colleges to develop in their students. Interestingly, a similar survey had been taken in 2007, and the top three answers were teamwork, critical thinking, and communication. The top answer in 2010 was none of the above. As if to demonstrate how fast the business climate shifts, the CEOs selected creative thinking as their top choice (Kern).

Would we argue that the ability to apply creative thinking is the most important skill on which higher education needs to focus? No, but we would say that it is a necessary complement to today's emphasis on critical thinking, and that the two bundled are a key survival skill.

And just as important as the skill development is the awareness of it. One goal of this book is to make you **metacognitive**. We want you able not only to apply creative *thinking*, but at least in the beginning to be aware that you are intentionally doing it. When you first started building Legos, you probably followed the direction to complete the fire station and the airport, but after a while you had internalized the basic process so that you could design and construct the LegoMall on your own. And when you took piano lessons, the more you improved through basic drill, the easier it was to improvise new riffs on familiar tunes. In the beginning you think about every step in detail, but with practice you learn to shoot the jumper without reminding yourself to square your shoulders to the basket, point your elbow toward the target, and follow through till you end up with an arm in the gooseneck formation.

And now a caveat. This book is not subtitled "An In-Depth Guide to Everything You Ever Wanted to Know about Creativity." If that's the book you want, we suggest you check out *The Cambridge Handbook to Creativity* or a Pysch textbook written for Ph.D. candidates. To the contrary, our book is an entry-level summary of the major facets of creativity designed for a general audience. As such, we have followed the advice of science genius, Albert Einstein, who is given credit for saying (although no one can find where), "Make everything as simple as possible, but not simpler." For those in the arts, we might have cited Thoreau's advice in *Walden*: "Simplify. Simplify. Simplify." In truth, we just want to acquaint you with the field of creative thinking, and if you like the taste, you can satisfy your hunger in other places.

Another caveat about this book. Take a good look at its title and its subtitle: *Introduction to Applied Creative Thinking: Taking Control of Your Future*. The emphasis in both the title and subtitle is on action. If you look carefully at the subject matter, it's not just **Creative Thinking**, but **Applied Creative Thinking**. In other words, we don't want you just to know some basic principles, but to be able to use them, to apply them to your everyday life. The phrase "Applied Creative Thinking" was carefully chosen because of its acronymic value—we want you to **ACT**. And we firmly believe that if you can add creative thinking to your collection of other skills—critical thinking, communication, research, and teamwork—you will have a better future even if you don't enter the business world for which IBM conducted its survey.

As you read on in this book, you'll find that after we define applied creativity and then demonstrate its importance, we're going to help you develop your creative thinking skills as an athletic coach would. Take baseball, for instance. To teach you to become an effective pitcher, we would first break the delivery position into its various skill points. After you mastered each point, we would gradually start putting the stance, the wind-up, the pivot, the thrust forward, and the throw together. Unless you are mechanically sound, you can't fire fastballs or deceive hitters with curves, sliders, and change-ups.

A major difference, however, between sports training and learning to think creatively is that the latter's skills are not necessarily sequential. Sometimes **brainstorming** (What's that? Read on.) will get you where you need to go, while other times you may find yourself frozen and need a **perception shift**. At times, simply pitching your idea to an engaged listener can completely change your perspective on a pressing problem. That is, engaged and sustained collaboration can serve as a catalyst for transformative experiences. Ultimately, perhaps, that is the most difficult thing about applying creative thinking—not just recognizing you need to employ it, but figuring out which skill(s) to try.

For instance, let's suppose a friend is starting up a business and needs help in coming up with a marketing logo and slogan that interlace—a sort of "slogoan."

Where do you begin?

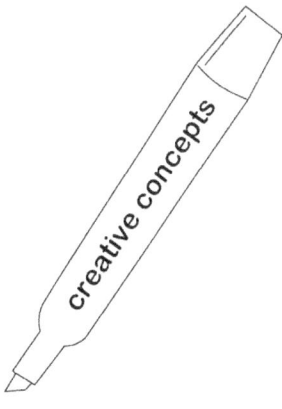

Creative Concepts

- **Convergent Thinking** is deciding on the right answer to a problem

- **Divergent Thinking** is a process wherein many ideas are generated in order to arrive at a solution.

- **Metacognition** is an awareness by which one intentionally thinks about thinking.

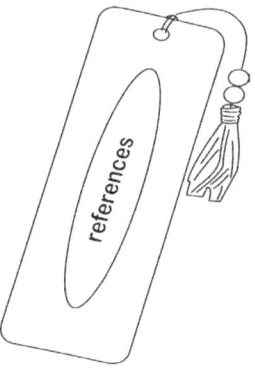

References

Kern, Frank. "What Chief Executives Really Want." *Bloomberg Businessweek* 18 May 2010. Web. 20 Oct. 2011.

What Is Applied Creative Thinking?

Let us retell an old parable about a wiseman who tested three of his students by sending them into the forest. Blindfolding them, he told them they would encounter beasts and they were to report to him what the beasts were like ... using only their sense of touch.

The first, who had chosen the path of the artist, claimed, "The beast is huge, and it feels like smooth rocks that have remained beneath the rushing waters since the dawn of time."

The second, who desired to be a farmer, testified, "The beast is huge, and its skin has the feel of a field that has been sun-dried for all of eternity."

The third, who was training to be a warrior, reported, "The beast is huge, and it must be fearsome because it feels like the spears of an army."

"This is strange," said the wiseman. "All of you have touched the only creature out there, yet you all describe something different. How can this be?" With that, he removed their blindfolds and pronounced, "Behold the beast!"

All three students stared at an elephant.

"You," said the wiseman to the first, "touched its tusks. You," he said, turning to the second, "brushed its skin, and you, number three, felt its teeth."

"What is the point of this experience?" chimed all three in unison.

You're probably asking the same question.

As you remember from the Introduction, **Convergent thinkers** seek a single point—**divergent thinkers** realize the story opens itself to multiple interpretations. The point is that there is no single point. For instance, the point of the parable might be that people interpret things through their individual perception of the world. Thus, the would-be warrior perceived the world through weaponry, the farmer through contact with the good earth, and the artist through aesthetics.

Take a minute to develop your own narrative of the parable's significance. When you first read it, was there some glimmer of meaning that you noticed? If so, go with it.

One meaning for us relates to the chapter's title. Since we are trying to provide a definition of creative thinking, the parable brings to mind that thousands of such definitions exist out there. Take another minute to Google "creativity definition" and see how many hits you get. And if you start to read over the definitions, you'll find that each field/discipline offers a slightly different focus on the subject. In later chapters we'll explore some of the major ways that business, science, and the arts delineate creativity.

In addition, creative thinking theorists tend to regard the field from four different perspectives, commonly called the Four Ps (Rhodes):

- The Creative Process
- The Creative Person
- The Creative Press
- The Creative Product.

The **Creative Process**, which is the emphasis of this book, consists of those learned skills that innovative thinkers employ. Some theorists have tried to divide those skills into generative and judging phases, while others have suggested that each phase has subsets. Others have suggested that skills follow a predictable pattern, while some disagree and point to various inter-related skills being available, but not all are used all the time. Most theorists believe in the notion of **recursiveness**—i.e., that whatever the process used, it is not a one-time thing, but something to which the thinker continually returns.

For instance, poets do not utilize the exact same mental process with every poem written. Sometimes they begin with a powerful emotion, an especially strong sense impression such as smell, or an image that overwhelms them. As they write, poets who rhyme return to the basic verse pattern, be it something as simple as ABAB or as complicated as a villanelle. Free verse poets tend to return to dominant images or even singular words. In Poe's famous "The Raven," he uses almost all of the above, constantly returning to his regular rhyme scheme, the visual image of the raven, and the repetition of the word "Nevermore."

The **Creative Person** is the focus of studies that examine those personality traits that produce a creative thinker. Most agree upon several of these traits, such as knowledge of the subject and a motivation to do something with the subject. Many suggest that the personality type most contributive to creativity is the *rebel, independent thinker, or outsider*, the person who as the starship Enterprise can leave known worlds behind and "boldly go where no one has gone before." When Charlie was growing up, his father more or less defined that outsider role by saying to him, "Son, if you spent as much time trying to play the game as beat the game, you'd be better off."

Creative persons are essentially *risk-takers*, whether it's being out driving and willing to try a shortcut home or taking a course not in your major just because it sounds kind of interesting.

Creative persons have a deep *love of ambiguity*. They are fine with alternatives. They can revel in the fact the reader doesn't know which door the princess' suitor selected in Frank Stockton's Classic "The Lady, or the Tiger," whether Robert Frost's persona took the road not often taken or the traditional route, or what really happened in the final episode of *Lost* when Jack led the flock toward the light.

Creative persons tend to be *energetic and inner-motivated*. They complete that difficult Sunday *New York Times* crossword puzzle though it takes hours and they are getting paid with nothing but personal self-satisfaction. They stay after class to help the instructor save a new contact list to her computer. They wake up in the middle of the night to scribble down the seed of an idea that may never germinate.

Creative persons are more interested in *synthesis and significance than in the small details* (MacKinnon 308-9). When they write fiction, Charlie is more concerned with the large plot movements, while Hal worries about the detail from plot causality right down to grammatical transitions.

Creative Press is a term used to describe the environment that contributes to optimal creativity (truthfully, we think "press" is used instead of "environment" only because the inventor of the four Ps needed a fourth P, not an E). That environment could be your dorm room, your work place, or a classroom. No matter, the creative room has several characteristics: it provides necessary resources; if it's public, it offers positive co-workers and instructors. Recent studies have suggested other contributory features, such as proper temperatures (academia likes 72 degrees, whereas business favors something a little higher), and proper color (some need a shocking red to stimulate them, while others relax more in a blue room).

When Charlie and Hal were starting out in academia, they would teach two classes early, then head for the local McDonald's to feed their heads and stomachs. Getting away from colleagues and students (they still kept ample office hours) at the same time every day helped them focus on the task at hand—producing publishable fiction and literary scholarship for a publish-or-perish world. By visiting the house that Ronald built, they averaged over 20 publications per year for over 20 years.

A recent commercial for Jeep that uses the tag line "The things we make make us" is an excellent introduction into the fourth P, the **Creative Product**. The Jeep is an obvious product as were Hal and Charlie's published pieces. Theorists on the product obviously focus on the end result of the previous Ps—did the process, press, and person produce something tangible that is useful? Sometimes the end result/product might be a new process or environment.

Useful has many connotations. In the world of business, the sales of the product are the determining factor. Some of Charlie and Hal's fiction sold, but some just appeared in literary magazines, so what was its usefulness? Yes, it helped them achieve tenure, but did their fiction broaden and sharpen their readers' views of life or their critical articles enlighten people as to why the house of Usher really fell? People who study creative product have devised theories about the phases a product goes through (business tends to favor the term innovation over creativity and the product as an invention), but most are interested in figuring out how to measure the usefulness of the product.

Popular lore and even Daniel Pink's recent book *A Whole, New Mind* (2005) perpetuate the myth that creativity is a right-brained activity. As we'll discuss in a future chapter on what science is telling us about creativity, "right-brained" is not synonymous with creative.

Perhaps the most common cultural metaphor for creativity is thinking outside the box. The more people use that description, the more clichéd it becomes and ironically the less creative. But this metaphor is a good starting point. The more people think, even those who become critical thinkers, the more their thought processes become patterned—i.e., the box or the rut. Creative thinkers are able to transcend these patterns—hence, Arthur Koestler's famed definition of creativity as "the defeat of habit by originality." Unlike the students in the chapter's opening parable who tended to see things from their warrior/artist/farmer perspective, creative thinkers might offer an entirely different way of regarding the beast or even synthesize extant views.

Some theorists like to make a distinction between "Big C" creativity, which they attribute to geniuses such as Einstein and Da Vinci, and "little C" or ordinary creativity that can be developed in non-geniuses. Cremin, Burnard, and Craft see creativity as "possibility thinking," which includes seven habits of mind: posing questions, play, immersion, innovation, risk-taking, being imaginative, and self-determination. Warner defines creativity as any "human act or process that occurs when the key elements of novelty, appropriateness, and a receptive audience in a given field come together at a given time to solve a given problem." Koestler believes creativity "uncovers, selects, re-shuffles, combines and synthesizes already existing facts, ideas, faculties and skills" (120).

While problem-solving is a major use for creative thinking, when we analyze the thousands of creativity definitions, two traits stand out:

- Novelty

- Utility.

When we generate creative thoughts, we find ourselves growing. The root form of creativity is the Latin *creatus*, meaning "to have grown." Creative thinking is the seed of that growth process.

Creative Concepts

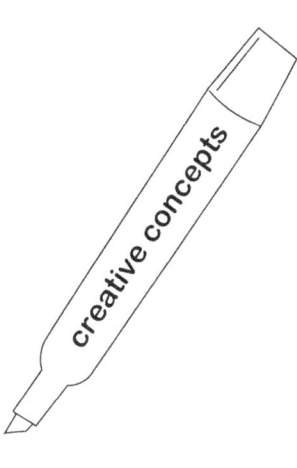

- **The Creative Process**, one of the four Ps, consists of those learned skills that innovative thinkers employ.

- **Recursiveness** is a process or a train of thought to which the thinker continually returns.

- **The Creative Person,** one of the four Ps, is the focus of studies that examine those personality traits present in a creative thinkers.

- **Creative Press**, one of the four Ps, describes the environment that contributes to optimal creativity.

- **Creative Product**, one of the four Ps, is an end result of creative thinking.

- **Big C Creativity** is a term often used to focus on the thinking of geniuses, while **little C Creativity** describes the creativity of non-geniuses.

Exercises

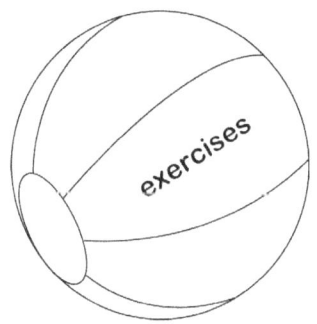

1. Provide another interpretation of the parable of the beast. Do parables support convergent thinking, divergent thinking, or both?

2. Keep a journal on a particular train of thought you have, perhaps one wherein you are trying to solve a problem. Do you notice recursiveness? Do you see a potential danger to thinking because of recursiveness? Albert Einstein is reputed to have defined insanity as "doing the same thing, over and over again, but expecting different results." Is "recursiveness" just another word for "insanity?"

3. Have you ever known someone who was considered an outsider? If so, what was it that person did that made him/her a rebel? Was it more than a fashion statement? Did that person actually think differently from the surrounding crowd?

4. Do a personality inventory. Do you have any of the traits that are considered essential for creative persons? If not, do you know the reasons you do not possess them?

5. After rereading this chapter, formulate your own definition of creativity.

References

Cremin, Teresa, Pamela Burnard, and Anna Craft. "Pedagogy and Possible Thinking in the Early Years." *Thinking Skills and Creativity* 1 (2006): 108-19. *WorldCat*. Web. 12 Oct. 2011.

Koestler, Arthur. *The Act of Creation*. New York: MacMillan, 1964. Print.

MacKinnon, D. W. "IPAR's Contributions to the Conceptualization and the Study of Creativity." *Perspectives In Creativity*. Ed. Irving A. Taylor and Jacob W. Getzels. Chicago: Aldine, 2005. Print.

Pink, Daniel. *A Whole New Mind*. New York: Penguin Books, 2005. Print.

Rhodes, Mel. "An Analysis of Creativity." *Phi Delta Kappan* 42.7 (1961): 305-31. Print.

Warner, Scott. *The Effects on Students' Personality Preferences from Participation in Odyssey of the Mind*. Diss. West Virginia University, 2000. Morgantown: WVU Libraries, 2000. *WorldCat*. Web. Oct. 2011.

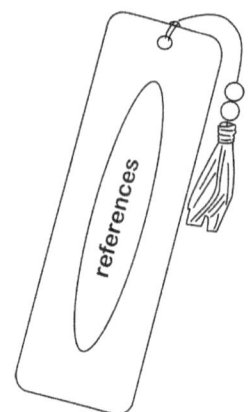

Rationale: The Critical Importance of Applied Creative Thinking

You're sitting in class and haven't said a word in half an hour. You find it harder and harder to pay attention. The student sitting in front of you is daydreaming; another is engrossed in Angry Birds on her iPhone. The stationary teacher in front of the room persists in a monotonic, blow-by-blow account of chemical equations. The lecture drags on for another half-hour until you think you can't take any more. After class, your friend turns off her iPhone and remarks on the stoic nature of the professor and the stereotypic nature of the classroom with its ...

- Rows

- Columns

- Dim lighting

- Monolithic Podium.

Yes, this hall has all the telltale clues of the standard classroom, but does learning really take place in such an environment? Think back to your favorite hobby. How did you learn to do it? Give yourself a minute to really think about it. Did you learn by simply memorizing information as if you were preparing for a test? How about by your mentor lecturing to you? Did you learn from taking quizzes? Does student passivity encourage learning?

NO! Principles of adult learning tell us that we learn through **interactivity**. That is, tests show us what we've memorized, but classroom environments that encourage us to learn by doing, modeling, and playing promote creative thinking skills. During the late 1990s, Lorin Anderson revised Bloom's taxonomy of learning. Interestingly, **creating** – that is a new product or point of view – replaced evaluation to reflect 21st-Century learning. Now, think back to that classroom. Take a minute to visualize that learning environment. What comes to mind? Inspiration and innovation? No, probably not.

That's because the classroom was built for order and control, not necessarily for the inspiration of novel and useful products. When was the last time that you walked into a classroom and the furniture was on wheels? Now, when was the last time your professor encouraged you to think with your hands and create something like a product or artifact? We argue that this time for creation is critical—or central—to the 21st-century classroom. Supporting learning as thinking with your hands, we encourage **play**; that is, making something useful out of ordinary items you have available to you. Keith Sawyer proposes that collaboration enhances learning and that we should carve out time for spontaneous creative thinking. He suggests that the typical meeting is too linear or structured and that there is value in **divergent thinking**. Sawyer posits that physical and intellectual constraints restrict the flow of ideas and that we should dedicate time for free-form thinking. Does that dark classroom with rows of chairs invite you to step outside your comfort zone to think about multiple and new ways of solving an old problem? We'd guess not.

Some points introduced earlier bear repeating. A typical college graduate will hold six to seven jobs in his or her career. It's likely that the job that you hold once you graduate doesn't yet exist. Daniel Pink argues that creative-style thinking will "increasingly determine who soars and who stumbles" (27). A 2010 IBM survey revealed that "chief executives believe that – more than rigor, management discipline, integrity or even vision – successfully navigating an increasing complex world will require creativity" (Tamasco). Indeed, the future belongs to creative thinkers. The new needs of employers in the 21st Century demand new learning environments that allow creativity to thrive.

This book is your opportunity to fully engage what is meant by creativity or to think critically about creativity. We focus on problem solving and design change. As a student, you've faced problems big and small, whether it's when to leave for class or how to put a fresh spin on your dinner for tonight or how to solve a societal problem like homelessness. This textbook is for those who want to make a positive change in their lives and even in the ways they engage information. We believe, as has been suggested, that students who possess and use creative thinking will emerge as tomorrow's leaders, solving infrastructure, budgetary, and employment issues with a fresh perspective; students who are willing to break from tired practices to design ones that transform organizations and cultures will rule. Future employers will look to recent graduates to fuse arts, sciences, cultures, and abilities. Creative thinkers excel at connecting ideas or creating solutions with little or no foundation or previous standard.

The traditional classroom, built with the "sage on the stage" model, provides a space where the professor talks and students listen. Traditional configurations don't promote creativity; that is, they don't make creativity an **intentional** part of the classroom learning experience.

On the other hand, creativity, according to Pink, involves **high-touch** and **high-concept** learning opportunities (Pink). High-touch refers to the ability to empathize, understand interpersonal communication, and grow beyond an everyday approach to solving problems, whereas high-concept refers to artistic beauty and combining what appear to be unrelated ideas into strong and innovative ones. High-concept and high-touch require skills in a number of areas, including **design**, **play**, **storytelling**, and **learning**.

The 21st-Century classroom embraces high-touch, high-concept learning. And the professor, well, he or she becomes integral to the learning experiences of students by becoming an active participant or co-facilitator in that process. In the 21st-Century classroom, the professor rarely teaches from the podium. Activities involve students and the professor learning together side by side. Desks are not set up in rows but clusters where students discuss key concepts, ideas, and questions. The majority of class time is spent with hands-on learning: high-touch. The professor creates intellectual and physical spaces where students tackle problems together—often in small groups—negotiating collaborative environments through discussions.

But what does this new methodology really mean for creativity? It means that classrooms should make creativity intentional. Students will engage numerous approaches to solving problems, and many will involve sustained **collaboration**. Students will have opportunities to try approaches that fit their learning style. Assignments will engage not only multiple lines of thinking but also multiple modes of communication—to include written, oral, visual, electronic, and nonverbal. Students will employ high- and low-tech resources that encourage them to **shift perspectives** about their projects.

This textbook is entitled *Introduction to Applied Creative Thinking*. In it, we share strategies for cultivating intentional and systematic competencies in students in order to develop creative leaders capable of solving emerging academic, business, and cultural challenges. While you're probably reading this book in a class that foregrounds creativity, these competencies can take you much further in your career than you probably think. Business leaders, as you learned in the Introduction, have cited creativity as the leading competency for future employees (Kern). This textbook provides the foundation for inspiring those creative practices. As you read, watch for clues and tools you can use to unlock ideas.

Key concepts we will explore include:

- Piggybacking

- Synthesizing

- Collaborating

- Convergent Thinking.

We will also take you through a process of learning involving:

- Making
- Risk-taking
- Improvising
- Playing
- Remixing
- Remediating
- Shifting perception
- Catching glimmers
- Diverging.

Applied creativity is generative and embraces possibility. At a practical level, it appears as visual and associative thinking. The best creative thinkers let ideas **evolve**. As ideas evolve, small changes and tweaks improve the idea from its original iteration. Creativity lies in refining the original idea. It is built on the previous version. At times, the most creative ideas emerge from changing direction, shifting focus from one angle or problem to another. Every problem has multiple solutions and avenues to get there. So, what attitudes foster creativity?

- Exercise curiosity
- Embrace challenge
- Adopt a problem-solving spirit
- Turn bad to good and challenges to opportunities
- Welcome mistakes and learn from failure
- Challenge assumptions.

These attitudes have little space to grow in the standard classroom. You, as the student, must be comfortable undoing learning as much as learning. When unlocking creativity, you must be prepared to let ideas go or combine them. Curiosity will drive 21st-Century learning experiences, fostered by the professor. This textbook serves as a guide, an invitation for you to break the rules, color outside the lines, and make new meaning. Here's the opportunity that you've waited for: to live the creative life and take control of your future.

So you want to be more creative? Well, reading this textbook is only a start. Much like the design of the ideal 21st-Century learning space, we've designed this textbook with space for your ideas. You're going to be writing, sketching, outlining, mapping, creating, and inventing all the time. We'll ask you to improvise while exploring new leadership roles. We'll use this experience to develop a common language. You'll play a key role in enhancing your creative experience. We ask you to think about the ways disciplines connect, intersect, and overlap. We also ask that you expose previously unexplored gaps to illuminate ways in which the creative mind can engage and confront challenges. The insights found here encourage you to become an interdisciplinary thinker. Here are some questions to ponder:

- How can poetry help confront hunger within your community?
- How can we use creative writing to learn mathematics?
- How can we use design to convey complex electronic diagrams?
- What might the next cellular phone look like?

The future belongs to creative thinkers who can express their ideas clearly and convincingly. Fundamental to the development of creative thinkers is cultivating intentional strategies. Can you articulate a creative process? What does a creative environment look like?

Are you ready to take the journey? To expand your thinking? To unlearn and relearn? Creative thinking skills will be the currency of the future. We look forward to taking this journey with you!

Creative Concepts

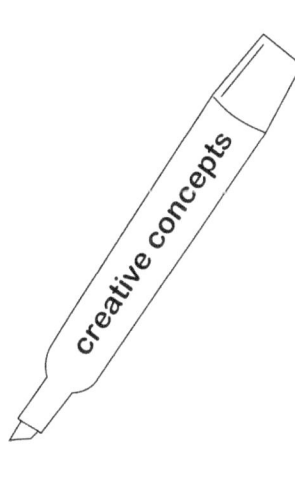

- **Interactivity** involves doing, modeling, and playing, which promote creative thinking skills.

- **Divergent Thinking** is a process wherein many ideas are generated in order to arrive at a solution.

- **High-touch** is Pink's term for the ability to empathize, understand interpersonal communication, and grow beyond an everyday approach to solving problems.

- **High-concept** is Pink's term for artistic beauty and combining what appear to be unrelated ideas into strong and innovative ones.

Exercises

1. What is your proposed field of study? Outline some reasons you think applied creative thinking could be useful in your field.

2. Give yourself a "Pink" Test. Do you have any aspect of "high-touch?" What about "high-concept?"

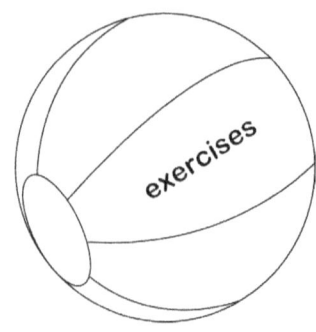

References

Anderson, Lorin, and David Krathwohl. *A Taxonomy for Learning, Teaching, and Assessing: A Revision of Bloom's Taxonomy of Educational Objectives.* New York: Longman, 2001. Print.

Kern, Frank. "What Chief Executives Really Want." *Bloomberg Businessweek* 19 May 2010. Web. 5 Sept. 2011.

Pink, Daniel. *A Whole New Mind: Why Right-Brainers Will Rule the Future.* New York: Penguin, 2006. Print.

Sawyer, Keith. *Group Genius: The Creative Power of Collaboration.* New York: Basic, 2007. Print.

Tomasco, Steve. "IBM 2010 Global CEO Study: Creativity Selected as Most Crucial Factor for Future Success." *IBM* 18 May 2010. Web. 5 Sept. 2011.

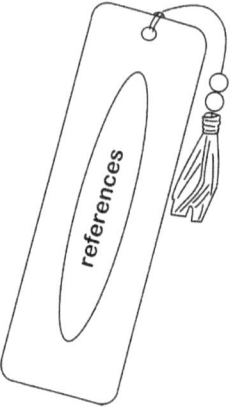

The Great Debate: Can Creative Thinking Be Taught?

While we were writing this book, we received an email from a faculty colleague who brought up a major issue that demanded an immediate response. In the interests of protecting the source, let's call the emailer Dr. Lud Dite, who began, "I'm sure you know, and if you don't know you need to learn, that there isn't any existing research that proves individual creativity can be taught. You're either creative or you're not (to be more accurate there are degrees of natural creative intelligence but it's not something which can be changed)."

Lud's position was news to us. After all, we'd had children who profited from the K-12 Odyssey of the Mind experience, and in our field of creative writing we had marveled at how poet Kenneth Koch had successfully helped New York City children in grades 3-6 create poems as he detailed in *Wishes, Lies, and Dreams: Teaching Children to Write Poetry*. Still, a critical mind must investigate and assess all claims, especially since if Lud were correct, then this whole book, *Introduction to Applied Creative Thinking,* would be based on a lie.

Perhaps synchronistically we picked up a recent issue of *The Chronicle Review* (part of *The Chronicle of Higher Education*), and the article's title leapt out at us: "Let's Get Serious about Cultivating Creativity." In it, Steven Tepper and George Kuh begin with, "Welcome to the Creative Era. To fuel the 21st-Century economic engine and sustain democratic values, we must unleash and nurture the creative impulse that exists with every one of us, or so say experts like Richard Florida, Ken Robinson, Daniel Pink, Keith Sawyer, and Tom Friedman." After expressing the democratic viewpoint of creativity, Tepper and Kuh emphasize it can indeed be taught: "creativity is cultivated through rigorous training and by deliberately practicing certain core abilities and skills over an extended period of time." The authors then detail those basic "abilities and skills":

1. "the ability to approach problems in nonroutine ways using analogy and metaphor;

2. conditional or abductive reasoning (posing 'what if' propositions and reframing problems);

3. keen observation and the ability to see new and unexpected patterns;

4. the ability to risk failure by taking initiative in the face of ambiguity and uncertainty;

5. the ability to heed critical feedback to revise and improve an idea;

6. a capacity to bring people, power, and resources together to implement ideas; and

7. the expressive ability required to draw upon multiple means (visual, oral, written, media-based) to communicate novel ideas to others." (B13)

In fact, higher education may be the last chance before the business world to teach these abilities and skills. According to the Robinson Report, at age 5 a child's potential for creativity is 98%, but by adulthood that potential had gone like a runaway elevator to 2%.

The evidence that proper instruction enhances creativity is mounting. Australian researchers Erica McWilliam and Shane Dawson state, "There is now a platform of research and scholarship that is making it possible to foster small 'c' creativity through sustainable and replicable pedagogical practice. ... At its core, creative capacity—the ability to 'move an idea from one state to another' (Jackson 2006b, p. 8) can be facilitated by the development of skills and capacities that allow optimal performance in and with the complex social and cultural forms emerging an effect of new interactive technologies. ... creativity is a skill that can be developed as a result of specific implemented pedagogical practices" (634-636). Robert Sternberg and Wendy Williams claim, "Creative work requires applying and balancing three abilities that can be developed. ... Encourage and develop creativity by teaching students to find a balance among synthetic, analytic, and practical thinking." In an article in *The Cambridge Handbook of Creativity*, Jeffrey Smith and Lisa Smith stress, "we think that the idea of mini-c creativity (Beghetto and Kaufman 2007) is so promising. It is what classroom teachers think creativity is in students, and furthermore it is an idea they can work with" (259). Smith and Smith also emphasize the importance of creativity in problem-solving instruction: "Students can be taught how to approach choosing creativity as part of problem solving both in terms of the process of generating ideas, and in terms of making the decision to utilize creativity as a natural part of their problem-solving repertoire" (260). Ronald Beghetto sums up this issue with, "Encouraging creative thinking while learning not only enlivens what is learned but can also deepen student understanding" (452).

Of course, education is not the only area in which creative thinking is being taught. American business has embraced creativity training, which accounts for what Kimberly Palmer refers to as "a growing number of businesses, organizations, and individuals trying to boost creativity, driven largely by the fact that today's economy requires it." As a result, she reports, creativity consultants hold "'gag sessions' where all kinds of ideas are encouraged and none are dismissed as stupid," conferences, retreats, and even online programs using Second Life. Matt Bowen, president of Aloft Group Inc. (a 28-employee marketing firm), responded to Kelly Spors' question, "Why are creative thinking and brainstorming technique so important to a small company like yours?" with "We found that most companies, and certainly some of our clients, tend to be very tactically driven. So what makes us attractive to our clients is that we offer the creativity that they don't feel they have."

No matter where it takes place, researchers into creativity instruction emphasize the importance of the environment. Tori Harang-Smith concludes, "If all individuals have the potential to be creative and if creativity is a process that can be dissected and therefore taught, then colleges and universities can work to create curricula, pedagogies, co-curricula programming and a general institutional environment to support creative development" (24). Just as important as the corporation's or the university's positive environment is that of the classroom; Kay Bull, Diane Montgomery, and Lynda Baloche conclude after a study that "a climate be established in which students feel safe and free to explore their creativity potential. This exploration should lead the student to an openness to creative experience, internal aptitude, and external environment. This openness, in turn, promotes curiosity and inquisitiveness, leading to insight and innovation" (89).

Yes, Virginia and Lud, creativity can be taught.

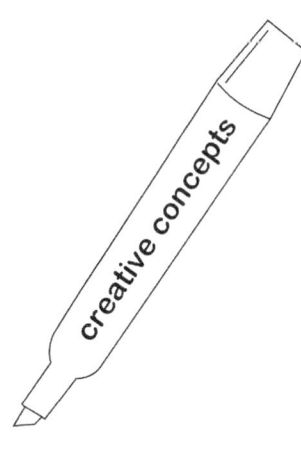

Creative Concepts

- Researchers today are convinced that creativity can be taught.

- Certain core abilities and skills can be developed and practiced in order to enhance individual creativity.

- Universities and the business world must create open, safe environments to promote creativity and innovation.

Exercises

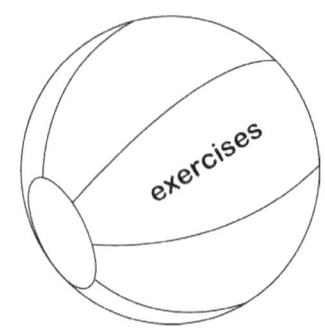

1. While you may not have done the research or experimented with the issue of whether creative thinking can be taught, examine your personal experience. In any course you have taken, have you gained an insight into creativity that you could then apply to some course of study? Have you ever been in an academic group where you brainstormed? Did you through the experience or instructor gain any transferrable insights?

2. Can you remember an incident when you were growing up that "taught" or encouraged you to be creative? Who was your "teacher?" What lesson did you learn?

References

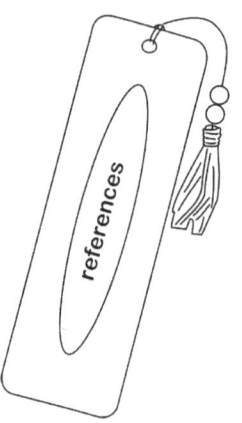

Beghetto, Ronald. "Creativity in the Classroom." *The Cambridge Handbook of Creativity*. Eds. James Kaufman and Robert Sternberg. Cambridge: Cambridge University Press, 2010: 447-63. Print.

Bull, Kay, Diane Montgomery, and Lynda Baloche. "Teaching Creativity at the College Level: A Synthesis of Curricular Components Perceived as Important by Instructors." *Creativity Research Journal* 8.1 (1995): 83-89. *EBSCOhost*. Web. 17 Oct. 2011.

Harang-Smith, Tori. "Creativity Research Review: Some Lessons for Higher Education." *Peer Review* 8.2 (2006): 23-30. *EBSCOhost*. Web. 13 Oct. 2011.

Koch, Kenneth. *Wishes, Lie, and Dreams: Teaching Children to Write Poetry*. New York: HarperCollins, 1980. Print.

McWilliam, Erica, and Shane Dawson. "Teaching for Creativity: Towards Sustainable and Replicable Pedagogical Practice." *Higher Education* 56 (2008): 633-43. *EBSCOhost*. Web. 13 Oct. 2011.

Palmer, Kimberly. "Creativity on Demand." *U.S. News & World Report* 30 April 2007: EE1-EE3. *EBSCOhost*. Web. 12 Oct. 2011.

Robinson, Ken. "The Creative Enterprise: Investing in the Arts in the 21st Century." The Arts Council of England. New Statesman Arts Lecture, London: 2000. Lecture.

Smith, Jeffrey, and Lisa Smith. "Educational Creativity." *The Cambridge Handbook of Creativity*. Eds. James Kaufman and Robert Sternberg. Cambridge: Cambridge University Press, 2010. 250-264. Print.

Spors, Kelly. "Productive Brainstorms Take the Right Mix of Elements." *The Wall Street Journal* 24 July 2008. Web. 19 Aug. 2009.

Sternberg, Robert, and Wendy Williams. "Teaching for Creativity: Two Dozen Tips." *Center for Development and Learning*, n.d. Web. 23 Sept. 2011.

Tepper, Steven, and George Kuh. "Let's Get Serious about Cultivating Creativity." *The Chronicle Review* 9 Sept. 2011: B13-B14. Print.

Myths of Creative Thinking

So if creative thinking is so important, you're probably asking about now, why don't more people, including your instructors, use it more often? First, any kind of thinking is difficult. There's a good reason that Rodin didn't fashion a sculpture called "The Daydreamer." Second, formal education has placed a premium on critical thinking, which teaches a patterned approach whether assessing for logical fallacies or employing the Foundation for Critical Thinking's "Elements of Thought," and many people find these patterns constraining. Third, creative thinking is also very misunderstood. In fact, many myths have grown up about creativity, myths that need dispelling.

Let's start by admitting the obvious: some people, whether by nature, nurture, or some combination thereof, have a tendency toward creative thought. In addition to the "usual suspects" who appear on every all-star list of creative geniuses, groups have been extremely influential toward developing creativity. During the 1860s, for instance, a core group of French Impressionist painters—Monet, Bazille, Renoir, and Sisley—held weekly meetings in Paris cafes, gradually extending their circle to include Pissarro, Manet, Degas and later non-painters such as Zola. In the early 20th Century Ransom, Tate, Penn Warren, and Davidson met together in Nashville, forming an influential group of poets and literary critics known as the Fugitives.

Myths, especially those supposedly formed by the level of science of the day, can actually impede creative thinking. In Columbus' day, for instance, the myth of the flat earth impeded physical exploration of the oceans, and those who did not subscribe to the earth-centered Ptolemaic theory of the universe could be burned as heretics.

Today most of the myths blocking creative thinking are not as deadly, but in terms of individual and cultural progress, they can be just as dangerous.

Creativity demands a high IQ. Actually, researchers have found no correlation between your being asked to join Mensa (the high IQ society) and your ability to create. However, creativity functions best when the user has a deep knowledge base of the subject to which the creative thinking is being applied.

Creativity is reserved for various kinds of artists and scientists. Yes, Shakespeare and Einstein were creative, but what about the person who invented Post-it notes or the first football kicker who tried to hit the pigskin not head-on but sideways like a soccer star?

Creativity is a lucky act. Maybe Newton wouldn't have figured out his laws if he hadn't been watching apples fall from trees, but one theory claims that creativity is the result of hard work. Ever have a coach, a teacher, or a parent tell you that practice makes perfect? Actually, it's not just random but deliberate practices that make you good at music so that you can write a symphony or at hoops to allow you to figure out and accomplish a never-before-seen dunk. In fact, the theory of **deliberate practice** argues that you need 10,000 hours of this dedicated activity to develop any skill to a high level, and that theory certainly applies to creativity. So maybe Newton's discovery was the product of years of study.

Creativity is fed by alcohol and drugs. If that's true, how can kids who have had no exposure to either narcotic write some excellent poetry? Certainly the Poes and Jim Morrisons have used narcotics to open creative doors, but we'll never know if they would have flourished without these stimulants.

Creativity happens only in solitude. Then how do you explain some of the great collaboration in history, such as the Bible, The Federalist Papers, and even The Beatles?

I can never be creative. We could tell you that with that attitude you'll never be creative, but that too is a myth. Problem solving through creative solutions is part of our evolutionary genes. Our ancestors had to be creative to figure out how to start a fire when necessary, how to carry water over great distances, and how to move heavy loads.

Creativity happens only under the pressure of what comic-book writer Stan Lee called the "dreaded deadline doom." While as a student you have no doubt been creative when you were under pressure to finish that due-tomorrow term paper, research has shown that more often production blocking occurs in tight situations. People who feel free have a better chance of producing something.

Others claim creativity is induced only by positive and negative rewards, that it happens solely in brainstorming sessions, that it needs total freedom or its opposite, a highly structured environment. History suggests, however, that no one size fits all, that what engenders creativity in one individual might not work for another.

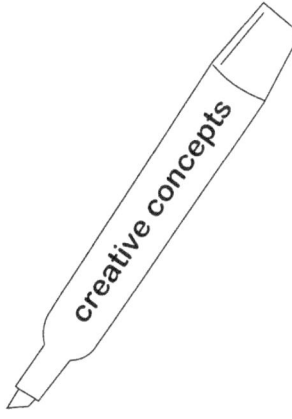

Creative Concepts

- **Myths** about creative thinking impede people's ability to create.

- **Deliberate Practice** is a theory that 10,000 hours of dedicated activity are necessary to develop high-level competency in a field, including creativity.

- Those environments that engender creativity can be different for different individuals; no one size fits all.

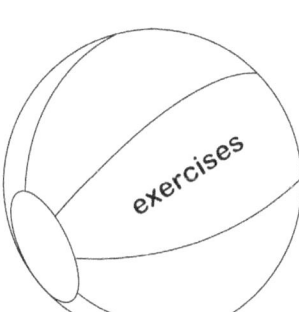

Exercises

1. When we wrote this chapter, we deliberately kept it short, preferring to introduce the concept rather than exhaust it. Can you identify one "new" myth about creative thinking that you believe and consequently is keeping you from developing your ability to innovate?

2. Choose a field in which you are pretty good or interested, be it comic book reading or Civil War history. What is your best estimate of the total amount of time you put into your love? Approximately what percent of that time did you really know what you were doing?

Enemies of Creative Thinking

"The creative capacities of generations of people have been sacrificed needlessly to an academic illusion."
                                            ***Ken Robinson*, Out of Our Minds 79**

Starting in kindergarten, we're taught to play, to use blocks to express ideas, to model behavior, to elaborate on stories, to sit on the floor, to allow our minds to wander. We make associations, see connections, and experience different types of communication. **Kinesthetic learning** takes command. At that age, students learn by doing.

And then we arrive at the door to our high school classroom. Upon seeing the classroom, it's painfully evident that rows of desks have consumed spaces once reserved for sharing ideas, expression. No longer are we encouraged to think with our hands but to memorize, recite, regurgitate as if, by this time, we've become some sort of mechanical receptacle of information. Have we tossed creative thinking out the window along with the "toys?" Have we shushed students just one too many times, as Trenia Napier suggests in her introduction to creative products (120)? Or do you learn best by being stifled?

Perhaps we need to revisit the colorful spaces of the elementary school classroom to generate creative insights for learning in higher education and beyond.

Once we enter the high school classroom, the days of learning by experience are over. We're taught to memorize, conform, and converge. Tests consume our educational experiences and even determine if we're eligible to go to the next level—college. Spaces, exercises, and experiences seem to highlight **convergent thinking**, while devaluing, or at least not acknowledging, the enriching and productive potential of **divergent thinking**.

Recently, we've witnessed an interest in deregulating "amateur creativity," as Lawrence Lessig says (254) in his discussion of remix. Regulations, as he would agree, stifle creativity. Lessig is primarily concerned with the remix of technological artifacts, but his point is one that certainly applies here, just one example of the rules that push against our creative spirit—in the classroom and beyond—as learners in the 21st century. In their discussion of creativity across the campus movement that took place at Clemson University, Patricia A. Connor-Greene, Catherine Mobley, Catherine E. Paul, Jerry A. Waldvogel, Liz Wright, and Art Young suggest that, "A crucial part of the process is the teacher's response to the student's production" (9). Judgment, that is to say, can stifle creative moments, just like regulations discourage **piggybacking** (building on others' ideas), which can be high or low-tech, or **remix**, if we're talking about the use of technology.

So, what are the enemies of creativity? Quickly, we'd say anything that constrains the free-flow of ideas in a way that doesn't provide adequate social space for them to ferment and for collaborators to respond, piggyback, or remix. But let's explore these enemies in a bit more detail.

As we've mentioned, rules can inhibit creative thought. Members of a group should be free to express ideas. Rules imposed in a creative environment can limit participants from sharing thoughts that could lead to breakthrough innovations. Rules restrict, while parameters can reinforce goals and keep creative sessions productive. Further, rules can isolate members of the group and can be divisive. Needless constraints—or those without purpose—kill creative thinking. Creative thinking lives and thrives in the divergent.

Creativity values connections, as connections help us see opportunities. Dead ends constrain, while actively seeking connections opens new opportunities for piggybacking. One point of view—a single channel of thought—inhibits divergent thinking. Similarly, we might look back to Lessig's argument that "amateur creativity" has merit. At some point in your college career, you're going to be asked to develop a creative product. In some cases, this product might take the form of a new perspective on an old idea. Quite often, though, the constraints that students become comfortable with in the classroom—and in their communication—are the same ones that doom them to a life of repetition. If creative artifacts—ones that encourage you to explore technologies and media connections—are produced using multiple modes of communication, which might include writing, oral communication, electronic communication, and perhaps an audio file or aural communication, then isn't monomodality an enemy of creativity? Let's think about it.

What if, when given an assignment, you had multiple choices for communicating your message? In the design process, you would need to consider your audience and then explore options for expressing your communication. The process of exploring those options is part of the creative experience. Now, let's shift our perspective just slightly to explore a few other opportunities.

Let's use, for example, Michael Jarrett's concept of jazz as a model for writing. Jarrett is interested in what he calls "jazzography" or "what people say jazz is" (2). What we appreciate about Jarrett is that he builds concepts on top of concepts; that is, he sets out in search of deeper meaning not by converging ideas, at least to start, but by diverging ideas to form new thoughts, theories, and practices that inform his view of literature and, in general, the world around him. He's able to "read" ideas and, at times, complex texts, through lenses that, let's just say, allow him to see the world differently. We'd argue that Jarrett is using **divergent thinking** here. He's not attempting to define jazz through writing. Moreover, he's interested in collecting perspectives. He has created a model. So, there's a major difference in the way we might approach "what people say jazz is" when compared to "provide a definition of jazz." One invites multiple perspectives, combining ideas, and making meaning, while the other seems to set the expectation for us—providing a standard of what the end product is going to look like.

The beauty of creative thinking is the potential for the unexpected. If you ask questions that you already know the answer to, what's the point of asking the question, right? We receive a different answer from a guiding question than we might for an open-ended question, which is a point that we often explore in the Noel Studio for Academic Creativity, a space that employs creative thinking in the development of communication skills among students. Guiding—with blinders on—sends us in one direction, while opening up the opportunities for multiple channels or several lines of thinking reveals multiple opportunities that you might not have seen before.

Jarrett's jazz example isn't the only one. Let's **expand** our thinking here by looking toward another example: the signature experiment (see Derrida's *Signsponge* or Scholes, Comley, and Ulmer's *Text Book*). Scholes, Comley, and Ulmer ask us to look at the visual nature of our hand-written signature: the strokes, slants, circles, and other features of our signed name on the page. Here, we're asked to make meaning out of our signatures. Now, we've tried this experiment before, but you can go ahead and take it for a test drive. Start by taking your name and designing meaning—or a practice for writing—based on its visual qualities. For instance, look at the first letter of your first name. Is it slanting forward? Perhaps the forward slant means that you should draft quickly. See what you come up with. What does your signature tell you about writing? Can you develop a writing practice based on the visual nature of your signature?

Creative thinkers, like Jarrett, have written many, many pages on this very topic. While you might have felt more confident in moving forward with a narrower topic and a bit more direction, this experiment requires you to draw on your creative-thinking skills.

The main enemy of creativity is a stifling environment—rows, unnecessary parameters, rules, regulations, and lack of encouragement. Creativity needs to be nurtured, and the wrong environment can inhibit divergent thinking.

A focus on convergent thinking without time for divergent thinking can be equally unproductive. Don't let a lack of confidence in pursuing ideas keep you from exploring relationships, as Jarrett has done, or making meaning, as we saw in the signature experiment.

Creative Concepts

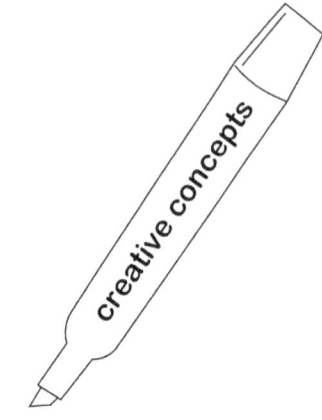

- Rules imposed in a creative environment (vs. parameters) can limit participants from sharing thoughts that could lead to breakthrough innovations.

- Creativity values connections.

Exercises

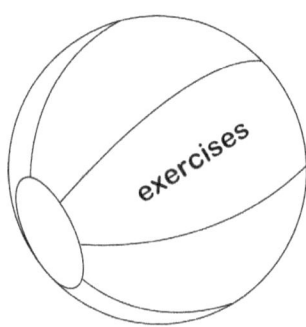

1. Let's continue an exercise suggested a few paragraphs earlier. The Latin phrase *nomen est omen* means "Your name is your destiny." If that notion is true, what does your name say about you? In any way, has your name already predicted a path your life has taken?

2. Choose a common expression of emotion such as "I love you" or "You love me." See how many ways you can express that emotion without stating it.

References

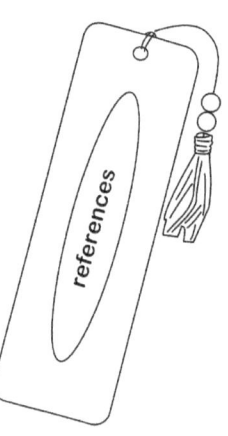

Connor-Greene, Patricia A., Catherine Mobley, Catherine E. Paul, Jerry A. Waldvogel, Liz Wright, and Art Young, eds. *Teaching and Learning Creatively: Inspirations and Reflections*. West Lafayette, IN: Parlor, 2006. Print.

Jarrett, Michael. *Drifting on a Read: Jazz as a Model for Writing*. Albany: SUNY, 1999. Print.

Lessig, Lawrence. *Remix: Making Art and Commerce Thrive in the Hybrid Economy*. New York: The Penguin Press, 2008. Print.

Napier, Trenia. "Introduction: Product." *It Works for Me, Creatively*. Eds. Hal Blythe and Charlie Sweet. Stillwater, OK: New Forums Press, 2011. Print.

Robinson, Ken. *Out of Our Minds: Learning to be Creative*. Westford: Capstone, 2011. Print.

Basic Creative Strategies: Shifting Perception

A couple of years ago, we had the opportunity to lead a group tasked with exploring creativity and its potential impact on the classroom. The focus was to be two-fold: how could instructors be more creative in their preparation and presentation and how could they elicit and nurture creativity in their students?

During the first meeting, one of our members dropped an unexpected bombshell when she said, "While I'm excited about studying creativity, I confess that I don't have a creative bone in my body." As we glanced around the room, we noticed several other members nodding in seeming agreement.

Perhaps you identify with our colleagues. When you encounter the concept of creativity, your thoughts immediately turn to those individuals whose creative triumphs are the stuff of history books, movies, and television documentaries. You may never achieve the stature of Archimedes, Beethoven, Marie Curie, George Washington Carver, Steve Jobs, or even that classmate in your comp section who always comes up with the innovative essay that earns the teacher's admiration and the A-plus. You can, however, discover that creative seed that dwells within each of us and nurture it to fruition by employing some strategies that have proven effective regardless of one's background or field of interest. We're so convinced of this truth that Rusty and the Noel Studio staff have named the room in EKU's new Noel Studio for Academic Creativity, in which students meet with each other and consultants to work on projects, the Greenhouse, because that's "a place where students bloom."

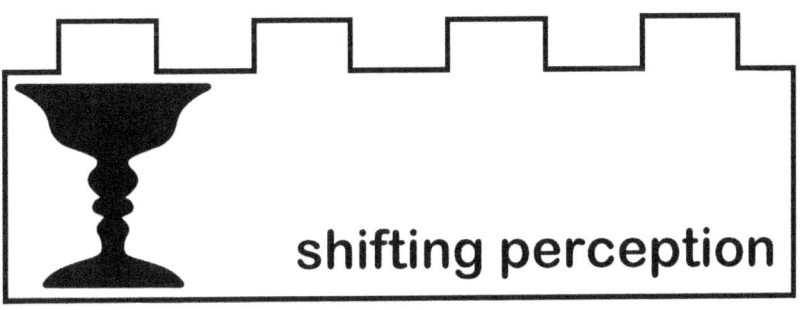

In the case of our zero-creativity colleagues, we realized that before they could become confident and productive members of the group, one thing they would have to undergo was a **perception shift**. You'll remember from the Introduction that this concept involved the ability to look at a person, idea, or situation from a new perspective. Our colleagues had to discard their previously held perceptions and learn to view themselves as creative individuals capable of not only understanding the creative process, but also employing it.

What steps did they—and you—need to take to achieve this highly transformative action?

- **Be open to the world around you.** The famous novelist Henry James once counseled writers to "be one on whom nothing is lost." Approach every situation with a willingness to see new things, to imagine possibilities. Whitbourne holds that "Openness to new ideas and a flexible attitude toward change are the essence of creativity." You never know when an experience might spark an idea. George DeMestral, for example, was walking with his dog through a field when he noticed that his companion was covered with burrs that seemed almost to jump on the dog's fur. On closer inspection, he noticed the unique hook-like structures of the burrs that allowed them to cling like tiny magnets. DeMestral's experience in the meadow led him to develop Velcro and dramatically change the clothing we wear. Or consider Malcom McLean, a trucking executive in North Carolina who was troubled by the excessive space and length of time it took to load trailers into the hold of the ocean freighters. One day, as he watched the roll-on/roll-off tedious process, he wondered what if there were a way to remove the wheels from his trailer and lift it on to the ship, where it could be stacked with others? That "way" led to the intermodal cargo crate that transformed the shipping industry.

  You may not come up with an innovative thought that changes the world or makes you a millionaire, but an openness to the myriad of opportunities around you can enrich your life and that of others.

- **Learn to network.** Very few, if any, individuals live in a vacuum. Every day we come into contact with people from various social, economic, educational, cultural, and religious backgrounds. Indeed, one of the greatest benefits of your college experience arises from the diversity of people with whom you'll come in contact. As Tepper asserts, "Creativity thrives on those campuses where there is abundant cross-cultural exchange and a great deal of 'border' activity between disciplines" (4). These relationships can offer you a tremendous spectrum of perspectives on any topic. To mine these riches, you need to connect with these differing voices, to listen to what they're saying, to learn what they have to offer. The American poet Walt Whitman expressed this idea in his "The Noiseless Patient Spider," in which he likens human connections to that process wherby the insect throws out filament after filament "out of itself" until one catches on to help construct the intricate web. Your "web" can be built through relationships you form in class, over lunch, at a ballgame, each allowing you a new and often different perspective on the world. And don't ignore research as a way of opening you to new views (isn't it interesting that we call that can't-live-without research instrument the world wide WEB?).

- **Don't be afraid to fail.** As he began his experiments on the 1000th version of the lightbulb, Thomas Edison was asked by a colleague if after 999 failures he wasn't getting a bit discouraged. To which Edison reportedly relied that, to the contrary, he was excited since he now knew 999 ways that didn't work, making his task that much easier. To be willing to view things from different perspectives is to be willing to risk failure. Cerf claims that "the freedom to fail" is one of the conditions that "give rise to innovation and facilitate its transforming effects" (A15).

Who isn't familiar with Stephen King, whose fiction dominated the best seller list for years? Few know, however, that the master of the macabre spent his early career experimenting with story after story as he tried in vain to break into publishing. Interestingly, his ground-breaking *Carrie* came as a result of his perception shift involving a combination of one incident at the high school where he taught and an article on telekinesis he read in *Life* magazine. Like the ingredients in gun powder, separately the elements were ordinary, but combined, they produced an explosion that thrust King into worldwide fame.

One of the most famous lines in movie history comes as Ed Harris, playing the head of the NASA team frantically working to bring the crew of Apollo 13 home safely, shouts, "Failure is not an option!" Ironically, however, the bulk of the movie is devoted to failure after failure as the team of engineers tries multiple options to keep the astronauts alive until a way to get their capsule through the earth's atmosphere safely can be discovered. Finally, one of the team members sees something others have missed, and success is achieved.

- **Don't hesitate to be different, even radical.** For years, Hal and Charlie had a poster in their office that pictured a cartoon turtle with an accompanying caption: "Behold the Turtle, Who Makes No Progress Without Sticking Out Its Neck." Their career as literary critics has been highlighted by a willingness to, as Emily Dickinson puts it, "Tell all the truth, but tell it slant." Much of their writing has flown in the face of traditional criticism, and many times their views have been rejected. Indeed, Fox admits that going against the flow can be "risky business," but claims, "sometimes, rules have to be broken to innovate." Once an article on Robert Browning the dynamic duo submitted to a journal was so controversial that the peer reviewer wrote in his rejection, "With names like Blythe and Sweet, are you sure these writers are serious?" We were, and our article later appeared in a more prestigious publication.

Certainly, more creative individuals than we have been criticized for their "different" perceptions. The annals of science are filled with accounts of ridicule and worse, received by those who challenged the accepted view.

Not until 1992 did the Vatican officially absolve Galileo of his heresy (for which he was imprisoned, tortured, and excommunicated) in holding that the sun was the center of the universe rather than the earth. And one has only to mention "The Monkey Trial" to call up memories of the controversy arising from a teacher named Scopes and his views on evolution.

- **Constantly ask "What if?" and "Why not?"** A new cable television program called *Alternative History* has an interesting premise: selecting various major events from history, the producers ask, "What if events had been different?" The first episode, for instance, treated the possible consequences if Germany had won World War II. How could that have happened? How would a Nazi victory have changed history? The answers provided a fascinating 30 minutes, and whetted interests for future episodes on such questions as "What if President Kennedy had not been assassinated?"

The book you are reading (as well as the course many of you are taking) came as a result of the three of us asking both "What if?" and "Why not?" questions. Working on another project, we kept running into questions about creativity and its place in education and the workplace. One day, one of us (we don't remember who) interrupted the flow of conversation to ask, "What if we created a minor in applied creativity that would incorporate courses from across the disciplines and give our students an opportunity to graduate with a value-added element in their resume?" After several weeks of research and visiting countless pros and cons, we concluded, "Why not?" Since our research had revealed an absence of texts suited for an introductory course in such a minor, we asked, "What if we wrote the book ourselves?" to which we said in unison, "Why not?"

Achieving perception shift is no magical act; it comes as the result of a mindset that allows you to view your world from a multiplicity of perspectives. Gomez holds that "In creative thinking, one deliberately searches for as many alternatives as possible" (38). This creative approach can be developed and refined—and anyone can achieve it to some degree.

By the way, our I-don't-have-a-creative-bone-in-my-body colleagues opened themselves up to the possibility of transformation and in the spring, following our fall meetings, contributed to both the creation and presentation of an interactive drama about creativity we staged for our state conference in education.

Creative Concepts

- **Perception Shift** involves looking at a person, idea, or situation from a new perspective.

- Definite strategies exist to help develop and refine perception shifting.

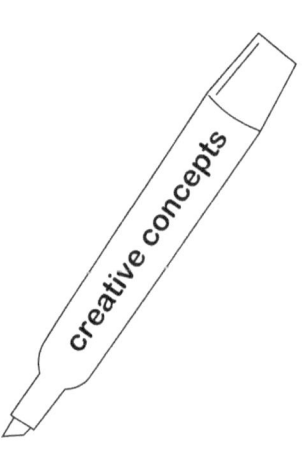

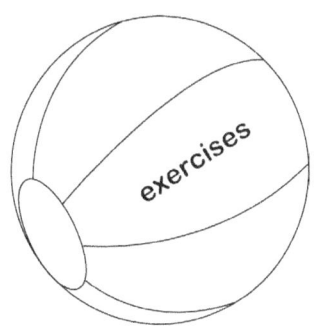

Exercises

1. Choose a popular fairy tale or legend. Assuming the role of one of the characters, recount the narrative from your point of view. How does your account differ from one told by another character? Why?

2. Choose a memorable event from your past. Ask yourself "What if" things had happened differently—how would your life have changed?

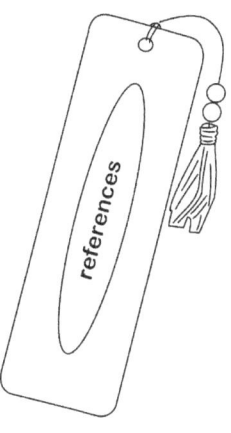

References

Cerf, Vinton. "How to Fire Up U.S. Innovation." *The Wall Street Journal* 12 Apr. 2011: A15. Print.

Fox, Mark. "The 10 Mental Blocks of Creativity." *Creative Thinking E-Book*. Slyasafox.com. Web. 3 Oct. 2011. <http://www.slyasafox.com/book/book13.html>.

Gomez, Jose. "What Do We Know About Creativity?" *The Journal of Effective Teaching* 7.1 (2007): 31-43. Print.

Tepper, Steven. "Taking Measure of the Creative Campus." *Peer Review* 8.2 (Spring 2006): 4-7. Print.

Whitbourne, Susan K. "Creativity and Successful Brain Aging: Going With the Flow." *Psychology Today* 23 Mar. 2010. Web. 3 Oct. 2011. <http://www.psychologytoday.com/collections/201109/do-you-go-the-flow/creativity-and-successful-brain-aging-going-the-flow>.

Basic Creative Strategies: Piggybacking

English scientist Isaac Newton once divulged what he considered the secret to creativity: "In order to see farther I have stood on the shoulders of giants." Whether investigating astronomy, optics, calculus, or motion, Newton found that building on the work of others furthered the cause of scientific discovery.

Newton's standing metaphor provides a powerful visual image of borrowing, but so does its other name, piggybacking. When we were kids, we used to piggyback by riding around on each other's shoulders, and more recently we may have been known to piggyback by using our cellphone/laptop to tap into someone else's internet service.

As a strategy in creative thinking, **piggybacking** (sometimes called hitchhiking) means something similar, borrowing.

And it's a strategy you're already familiar with because you've been taught to use it in basic research. Think of the term papers you've written over the years. In education, social sciences, and the hard sciences, after establishing your research hypothesis, you present a review of literature in the precise area in order to show its history and current thought. In writing about literature, you start with your thesis and then offer a summary of the criticism on the subject. In all fields the listing of previous research provides the proper foundation for the ideas you wish to erect.

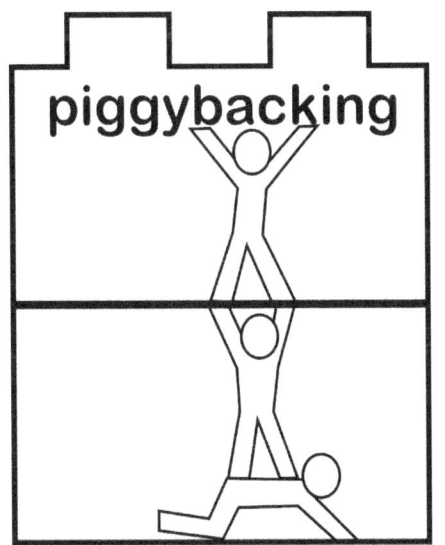

Sir Ken Robinson states, "Most original thinking comes through collaboration and through the stimulation of other people's ideas" (Azzam 25). The main point is that ideas don't spring forth *ex nihilo*—i.e., from nothing. New thoughts develop from what we already know. While Air Supply may have been able to make love from nothing at all, for creativity you need knowledge.

In fact, isn't all new knowledge an extension of old knowledge?

Consider the genesis of some familiar things in our world today. Aren't space shuttles variations on airplanes? Take a look at your iPod. Now look up the Sony Walkman on the internet? Do you see the parentage? Got a copy of Stephen King's *Carrie* lying around in book or DVD form? The master of the macabre claims that he got the idea for his telekinetic prom queen from an incident that happened while he was teaching at a Maine high school; at the same time he was reading an article on ESP in *Life* magazine. To create a novel, he simply grafted the unknown mental capacity onto a known real-life incident.

In *Borrowing Brilliance,* David Kord Murray summarizes the six steps to constructing a creative idea:

- Defining—Define the problem you're trying to solve.

- Borrowing—Borrow ideas from places with a similar problem.

- Combining—Connect and combine these borrowed ideas.

- Incubating—Allow the combinations to incubate into a solution.

- Judging—Identify the strength and weakness of the solution.

- Enhancing—Eliminate the weak points while enhancing the strong ones. (280-1)

Of course, poised at the center of the process is piggybacking. Interestingly, at the start of the process, Murray recommends "ideas": note the plural. At the onset of constructing an idea, it's important to borrow many possibilities.

However, one of Murray's pieces of advice may not be universally applicable. He also suggests that the ideas chosen be "similar," which is a difficult thing to judge. While the space shuttle and the airplane are both Things That Fly and the iPod and the Walkman are Portable Listening Devices, under what Jeopardy category would you put a high school prom queen and telekinesis? In his poem "Art," the 19th-century American writer Herman Melville notes that for art to be produced, "what unlike things must meet and mate." In other words, Melville emphasizes that in the non-scientific realm of art, often <u>dissimilar</u> things must merge to create a product such as a poem.

Hollywood has long understood piggybacking. In fact, when writers pitch television shows, they often use a type of shorthand referred to as "high concept," wherein the new product is very briefly described in terms of a previous hit. Thus, the megahit *Miami Vice* started on a cocktail napkin as "MTV cops," Dallas was begat from "*Romeo and Juliet* in Texas," and the short-lived and little-known series *Queen of Swords* was pitched as a "female Zorro." The process has the advantages of simplification and decreased risk much like the Tinsel-town tendency to remake certain movies every few decades.

So how do you go about borrowing? Research tells us that the major difference between "Big C" and "little C" creativity is the extent of the creative thinker's knowledge. A pianist who has devoted a life to music has a greater chance of creating something worthwhile than someone who has just mastered "Chopsticks." Perhaps you can combine Murray and Melville; start by borrowing things from allied fields, then move to less similar domains.

A few years ago Hal and Charlie were examining "The Fall of the House of Usher" in order to figure out an answer to the great critical debate on why Poe's fictional house fell. They started as traditional literary critics, assembling previous lit crit to see what the experts said. Once they had the amalgam distilled into some similar strains—aesthetic responses, supernatural solutions—even though they had analyzed the more traditional approaches, they were still dissatisfied. Finally, they tried a dissimilar field that led to a eureka moment. Synchronistically, at the time they were practicing literary critics accumulating tenure and reprints, they were also fiction writers getting paid to publish mysteries, and since Poe was the father of the detective story, they wondered what would have happened if Poe had sent his creation, the first fictional detective, C. Auguste Dupin, to the fallen structure of the Ushers. The result involved applying some creative thinking as they had to marry two very unlike genres – academic literary criticism and mystery stories aimed at the general public. The result, "The Case of the Fortunate Fall," created a new genre, fictional criticism, and led to a unique explanation as to the house's fall (we'd give you our solution, but that would be spoiling).

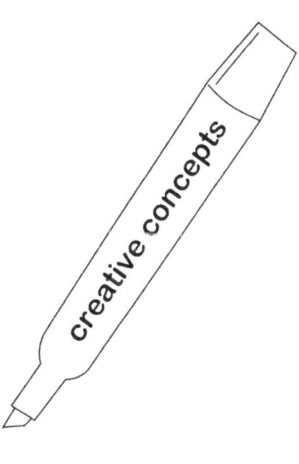

Creative Concepts

- **Piggybacking** is a creative strategy for borrowing old ideas from others in order to form new ideas.

- Piggybacking usually starts with similar fields and can spread to dissimilar ones, depending on the knowledge of the ideator.

- You've already practiced piggybacking when you wrote term papers for your classes.

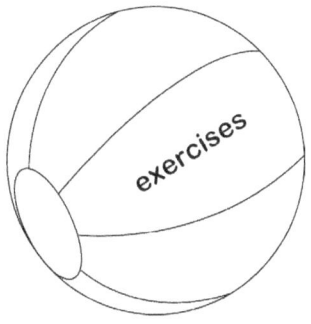

Exercises

1. Piggyback by finding an essay on something you enjoy, whether it's an academic subject, a hobby, or your favorite food. Add your thoughts, whether you use research or not, in order to build upon a viewpoint in the essay.

2. Have your class broken into groups of four or five. Choose a well-known fairy tale/legend for each group. Have each group add something to the basic story to "modernize" it (e.g., how much faster could the prince have found Cinderella if social networking existed?). Each group shares their revised story with the entire class and asks for further additions.

References

Azzam, Amy. "Why Creativity Now? A Conversation with Sir Ken Robinson." *Educational Leadership* 67.1 (2009): 22-26. *EBSCOhost*. Web. 18 Oct. 2011.

Murray, David Kord. *Borrowing Brilliance*. New York: Gotham Books, 2009. Print.

Newton, Isaac. "Letter to Robert Hooke." 15 Feb. 1676.

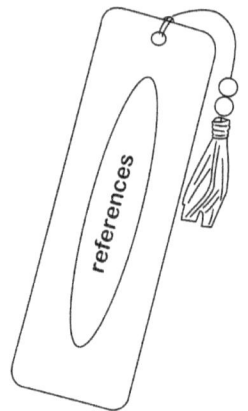

Basic Creative Strategies: Brainstorming

In the 1950s when advertising executive Alex Osborn introduced **brainstorming** as a process to enhance idea generation, he couldn't possibly have imagined the impact his strategy would have in the years to come. Even though subsequent studies have challenged its effectiveness (e.g., Mullen, Johnson, and Salas; and Furnham), brainstorming has maintained its position as the default technique for applied creativity whether the goal is an innovative consumer product, a persuasive political campaign agenda, or that dynamite destination for Spring Break!

Since you're probably not ready to star in a 3:00 a.m. infomercial or run for state senator, let's focus on the Spring Break decision. With your freedom from the tyranny of textbooks and teachers only a couple of weeks away, you and your buddies (we'll pick on the guys for this example) gather in your dorm room to make plans. Be honest—what is apt to happen? How many times have you been involved in what was supposed to be a brainstorming session that devolved into a shouting match or dissolved in total silence.

Why?

Perhaps Vincent Brown and Paul Paulus offer an answer when they point out that "unstructured groups left to their own devices will not be very effective in developing creative ideas." Without some type of structure, the chances that you guys will arrive at a decision that is satisfactory to all are almost zero.

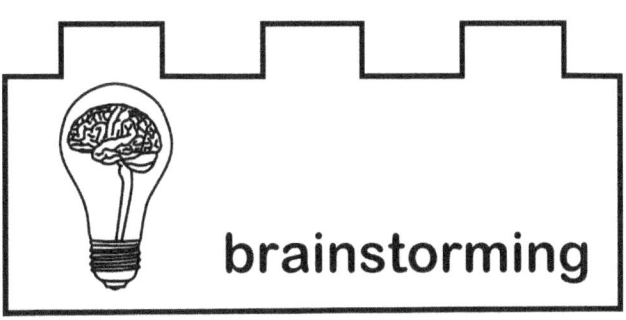

Research has revealed three major roadblocks to group creativity:

- **Production blocking** occurs because since only one group member can speak at a time, ideas are lost, people fixate on certain ideas, and some members censure themselves. Suppose your buddy Bob has already made up his mind that you're going to Daytona Beach, he'll drive his car, you'll leave Friday at 5:00 p.m., stay at the hotel his older brother told him about, and head home the next Thursday morning. Doesn't every group have one or two members who dominate the discussion?

- **Evaluation apprehension** results because some members of the group are afraid their suggestions will be negatively received, and for every Bob there's a Sam, who just doesn't have the confidence to express himself for fear he'll appear stupid. Even if he has something potentially valuable to contribute, he stays quiet and goes along with the group's (or Bob's) decision.

- **Free riding** or **social loafing** is a condition whereby some group members, for a variety of reasons, refuse to contribute to the group. What about Jim, who spends the entire session on his iPhone, seemingly oblivious to the conversation, then claims at the session's end, "I don't care where we go; just let me know?"

Osborn laid the foundation over 50 years ago when he prescribed brainstorming as a **process** involving four definite rules:

- Generate lots of ideas; quantity is initially more important than quality;

- Avoid criticizing any idea immediately; critiques can come later;

- Combine and improve on others' ideas; and

- Encourage "wild" ideas; anything is initially fair game.

Since the 1950s, Osborn's rules for effective brainstorming have been built upon by a number of research studies until a body of **best practices** has evolved that could make your Spring Break planning session truly productive.

- Brainstorming can be more effective when used in three stages: brainstorm alone, brainstorm with others, and brainstorm about your discoveries afterwards (Leggett, Putnam, Roland, and Paulus).

- Production blocking can be overcome (Barki & Pinsonneault).

- Groups need convergent thinkers (who tend to fixate on a single category in depth before continuing) and divergent thinkers (who tend to hopscotch through categories).

- Diversity of knowledge base promotes productivity (Paulus, Larey, & Ortega).

- Training in group idea generation can aid performance (Meadow, Parnes, & Reese).

- Setting a definite and challenging goal improves performance (Wegge & Haslan).

- Successful groups practice deep listening (Sawyer).

- Members need to beopen to perception shifts/new ways of looking at things (Larey & Paulus).

- Motivation is important to idea generation (Brown & Paulus).

Suppose that instead of getting together at the last minute to bicker about Spring Break, before going for pizza, you actually planned this session in advance, giving everyone the expressed goal of deciding when and where to go for the break, how to get there, where to stay, and when to return home. That way everybody could think about the choice **before** the gathering and have some ideas to throw out. At the session, everybody gets a chance to contribute without fear of ridicule, since all the ideas are accepted initially. In fact, remember Osborn; you **encourage** "wild" ideas.

Don't worry if Sam's ideas all revolved around where to stay, or Jim jumps around between transportation and time frame; your group can benefit from both **convergent** and **divergent** thinking. The fact that you came into the session with a well-defined **goal** and a **commitment** to that goal (we've got to get out of this place) gives you a head start toward success.

As the session progresses, be sure you **listen** carefully to what others say and remain open to **new ideas** they present; who knows, you might be able to build on something one of your buddies suggests. Again, you're fortunate that your group has such a **diversity** of backgrounds since the individual knowledge each brings to the session promotes productivity.

After an hour or so, you whittle down all the ideas until you have a plan. Panama Beach wins out over Daytona as the best destination in terms of distance and affordable lodging/food. Bob's car strikes a nice balance between looks and economy and certainly beats Greyhound or Delta for transportation. Sam kept coming back to where to stay since he's from Florida and knows the Panhandle well, and you win over the others concerning departure and return since they respect your organizational skills. After all, you were the one who set up the session.

In addition to keeping you from coming to blows and destroying a thriving friendship, your organized approach to creative brainstorming has successfully achieved your goal while at the same time allowing you to enjoy three benefits of effective brainstorming: (1) employment of specialization, (2) pooling of resources, and (3) increased decision acceptance (Furnham).

Happy Breaking!

Creative Concepts

- Brainstorming is a process involving several research-based practices.
- Roadblocks to effective brainstorming exist.
- Brainstorming affords several benefits in addition to achieving a goal.

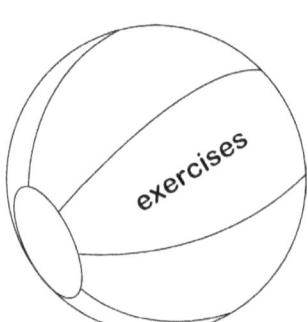

Exercises

1. Divide the class into groups (Class A and B). Tell Class A only that next session you will break them into three groups, each with the task of creatively solving a problem.

2. For Class B, provide the same basic information, but also tell them specifically what three problems will be treated and break them into three groups according to interest relative to the problems. Suggest that each individual give some thought to his/her group's issue before next session.

3. At the next class meeting, randomly break Class A into three groups and provide each with one of the problems. Then, after instructing the Class B group to use the best practices outlined in this chapter, have the groups "brainstorm" their issue.

4. Allow time for the groups to report out to the entire class. What differences are apparent in terms of results, individual and group satisfaction, group agreement?

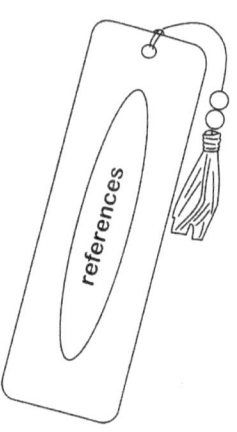

References

Barki, Henri, and Alain Pinsonneault. "Small-Group Brainstorming and Idea Quality: Is Electronic Brainstorming the Most Effective Approach?" *Small Group Research*, 32 (2001): 158-205. *EBSCOhost*. Web. 16 Oct. 2011.

Brown, Vincent, and Paul P. Paulus. "Making Group Brainstorming More Effective: Recommendations from an Associative Memory Perspective." *Creative Directions in Psychological Science* 11 (2002): 208-12. *EBSCOhost*. Web. 15 Oct. 2011.

Furnham, Adrian. "The Brainstorming Myth." *Business Strategy Review* (2000): 21-28. *WorldCat*. Web. 11 Oct. 2011.

Larey, Timothy, and Paul Paulus. "Group Preference and Convergent Tendencies in Small Groups: A Content Analysis of Group Brainstorming Performance." *Creativity Research Journal* 12 (1999): 175-84. *EBSCOhost*. Web. 19 Oct. 2011.

Leggett, K., Putnam, V., Roland, E., & Paulus, P. "The Effects of Training on Performance in Group Brainstorming." Paper presented at the annual meeting of the Southwestern Psychological Association, Houston, Texas, 1996.

Meadow, Arnold, Sidney Parnes, and Hayne Reese. "Influence of Brainstorming Instructions and Problem Sequence on a Creative Problem Solving Test." *Journal of Applied Pyschology* 43 (1959): 413-16. *EBSCOhost*. Web. 19 Oct. 2011.

Mullen, Brian, Craig Johnson, and Eduardo Salas. "Productivity Loss in Brainstorming Groups: A Meta-analytical Integration." *Basic and Applied Social Psychology*, 12.1 (1991): 3-23. *EBSCOhost*. Web. 19 Oct. 2011.

Osborn, Alex. *Applied Imagination*. New York: Scribner's, 1953. Print.

Paulus, Paul, Timothy Larey, and Anita Ortega. "Performance and Perceptions of Brainstorming in an Organizational Setting." *Basic and Applied Psychology* 17 (1995): 249-65. *EBSCOhost*. Web. 20 Oct. 2011.

Sawyer, Keith. *Group Genius: The Creative Power of Collaboration.* New York: Basic Books, 2009. Print.

Wegge, Jurgan, and S. Alexander Haslam. "Improving Work Motivation and Performance in Brainstorming Groups: The Effects of Three Group Goal-setting Strategies." *European Journal of Work and Organizational Psychology* 14 (2005): 400-430. *GoogleScholar*. Web. 11 October 2011.

Basic Creative Strategies: Glimmer-Catching

Ideas are like dreams—we have a hard time remembering even the best and worst of them. In the Chippewa culture the dreamcatcher is a handmade "spiderweb" about the size of a drink coaster crafted out of a hoop, natural lacing material like bark or vines, and even yarn. Hung over beds, the dreamcatchers were charms intended to keep children from harm by filtering out the stuff of nightmares and collecting the good.

Ah, that we all possessed dreamcatchers to capture key ideas or portions thereof that too often elude us. Just like words on the tips of our tongues, solutions to problems often dance just outside our full notice. A glimmer is a dim light, sometimes flickering, always in the distance, and just barely perceptible.

In creativity, a **glimmer** is that idea flashing in the corner of your eye or lurking in a darkened recess of your mind that you can't quite grasp or pull into your full consciousness.

One problem writers of all types have is the necessity of a dual focus. While taking pen to paper or word to processing, the writer must concentrate on what is going down permanently at the pen or finger tip, yet while so focused, the writer often sees the glimmer of the next idea like a train signal far down the track. However, flip the mental switch and focus afar, and the writer can lose sense of the present thought. In fact, one wonders how the old quill writers ever put a single thought down while trying to simultaneously keep ink on the quill and not tear the paper. However, all you have to do is walk into a library to realize that economists and essayists, poets and playwrights were all able to accomplish this task.

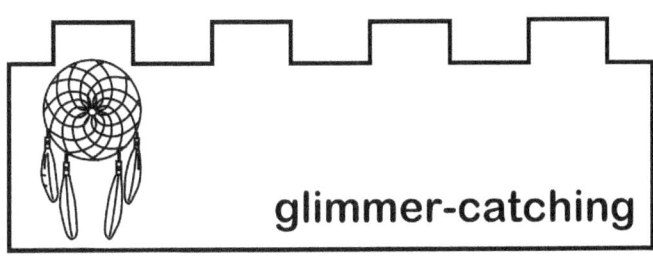

The notion of the glimmer fascinates us, whether in pop culture of serious art. Remember *The Glimmer Man*, the movie where Steven Seagal plays a spy who was so adept at stalking his victims in the jungle, all they would see was a glimmer before he dispatched them? Wait a minute, wasn't that the plot of *Predator*, too? Sometimes the creative artist intentionally uses the glimmer strategy so that we don't see the light immediately. For example, in poem #1129 Emily Dickinson exhorts us:

> Tell the truth but tell it slant
> Success in Circuit lies
> Too bright for our infirm Delight
> The truth's superb surprise
> As lightning to the Children eased
> With explanation kind
> The truth must dazzle gradually
> Or every man be blind—

What Dickinson suggests is that art should suggest. Rather than hit you over the head with obvious parables, the artist should provide the audience with a glimmer and let them work toward the "Truth."

Still, our focus here is on another problem: how does a creative mind become better not at creating a glimmer, but first recognizing it?

One, as Henry James advised a young writer in "The Art of Fiction," "Try to be one of the people on whom nothing is lost" (648). The more you are aware of your surroundings, especially the field you are in, the easier it is not to get lost. Here the concepts of deliberate practice and expertise definitely come into play as those who are experts and those who have rehearsed have better odds. Major leaguers catch more fly balls than Single A players (note that even this analogy depends upon some baseball expertise). Charlie and Hal once wrote a ground-breaking explication of Poe's "Berenice" because they were truly listening to each other. In the story the main character has developed a fascination with pulling the teeth from his buried loved one, and the critics couldn't figure out why. While Hal and Charlie were tossing around theories, one of them opined that Berenice was perhaps a vampire and the main character was worried she was going to rise from the grave, bite him, and turn him into a vampire. After a good laugh, Charlie and Hal, both fans of pop culture who believed that Poe's "The Fall of the House of Usher" was definitely about vampires, started looking at the evidence, and there was more than enough to make a good case.

Two, **try keeping a written or an electronic journal**. William Wordsworth found it easier to write after his trips through the Lake District of English because he had the journals of his sister, Dorothy, who followed him and took down what Wordsworth and his walking companion, Samuel Taylor Coleridge, mused about. In Hollywood every writers' room for a TV series has a production assistant whose job it is to transcribe all the words being tossed out. Later the ideas will be printed out and used as the basis for scripts. You can easily buy electronic gadgets that will record your sudden ideas whether you are pushing a shopping cart or waking up with a brainstorm. Henry James often wrote scenarios for his novels that were longer than some paperback novels. One trick we've learned is that if a thought occurs about something you wish to get to in the future ... collaborate [see, we just had a glimmer] ... just write/type it into your current sentence as a reminder.

Of course, an even better but difficult to practice strategy is that when you catch a glimmer, instead of making notes, work immediately on the project. Unfortunately, reality constantly intrudes with the demands of the immediate—get the kids dressed, take that online test now, repair that broken window. Coleridge claimed that the reason he never really finished his masterpiece "Kubla Khan" was that a stranger knocked on his door while he was in the throes on inspiration—a/k/a opium dream (for a discussion of this account, see Lowes). To counter the tyranny of the now, try working ahead; if your To-Do Lists are short, you'll find it easier to work on the fresh idea that sets in front of you like a butterfly.

Three, **collaborate and listen.** One advantage of collaborating is that most everything gets talked out. If you truly listen and take notes on what others are saying, you often find a platform for your own thoughts. Of course, collaborating (the subject of its own chapter) has its downside as while you are listening, it's difficult to be writing or follow a trail of your own thoughts.

Four, **try to spot the outlier in a group.** Remember that Sesame Street song, "One of these things is not like the other,/One of these things just doesn't belong?" Have you ever seen Bruegel's "The Fall of Icarus?" The landscape seems an edenic pastoral painting of a hillside, the sun just over the water, and a ploughman and a shepherd going about their daily business. However, on closer inspection Icarus' legs can be seen in the water near the ship. While the picture is often interpreted as demonstrating human indifference to the suffering of others, it also reveals that Icarus is the outlier, the one part of the painting that is not an every-day incident. When you are thinking creatively, pay close attention to the thing that is different.

On a more practical level, Charlie has been helping one of his sons play *This Old House* by building an inside secret door. The hinging was easy—the locking mechanism, difficult. Finally Charlie and his son went out to Home Depot and bought six different magnetic catches. They tried placing the mechanism on the door, then on the jamb, but with no success. Finally they noticed they were always placing the catches half-way up the door/jamb, and one of them said something about locating the catch at the top or bottom. They both heard the comment, tried the top, and because the angle was different, success resulted.

Five, **work on glimmers**. Too many times we dismiss the partially-formed idea as not good enough or not worth developing. So what if it doesn't work out? If nothing else, you've honed an effective creative strategy.

Creative Concepts

- A **glimme**r is that out-of-focus object in the corner of your eye, barely perceptible sound, or fuzzy idea that is the start of a larger idea.

- Glimmers can flash in a variety of situations and a variety of forms.

- Glimmers should be recorded so as not to be lost.

- Glimmers should he worked on as soon as possible after capturing them.

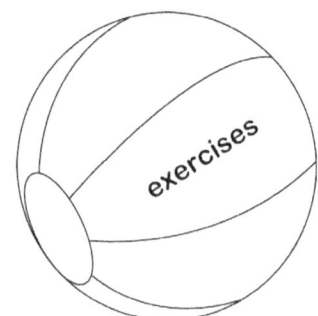

Exercises

1. Pick a problem you would like to solve, but instead of just thinking about possible solutions, make some shorthand notes with all your solutions. When you have finished, study your list. First, notice your solutions. Most people come up with the easiest/most obvious solutions first. Second, check your list for hints of things you have discarded. We tend to get rid of things that don't offer immediate solutions. Three, ask yourself if any of these "hints" suggests something else, something you might develop down the road.

2. Sleep is a very effective way of generating glimmers. Charlie once swore that in the middle of the night he had a brilliant idea for the next great American novel, but he couldn't remember even a glimmer when he awoke. Therefore, place a pad and pencil or an electronic "secretary" beside your bed. Think about a problem needing a solution before you go to bed. The second you awake, record any thoughts in your head, even if they don't seem related.

References

James, Henry. "The Art of Fiction." *Anthology of American Literature*, II. 7th ed. Eds. George McMichael, et al. Upper Saddle River, NJ: Prentice Hall, 2000. 642-56. Print.

Lowes, John. *The Road to Xanadu*. Boston: Houghton Mifflin, 1927. Print.

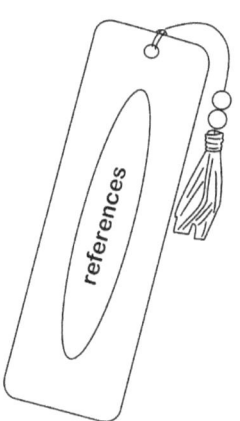

Basic Creative Strategies: Collaborating

Financial experts claim that one of the most powerful tools in investing is compound interest. For example, a $100 investment allowed to compound at a rate of 8% will double in just nine years (we realize that for an 18 year old, nine years seems an eternity, but, trust us, over a lifetime it represents a small chunk of time). Applied creativity has an equally powerful tool: collaboration. While individuals such as Shakespeare and Einstein get most of history's applause for their creative genius, ignoring the results of what Keith Sawyer calls "group genius" is impossible. Where would music be without Gilbert and Sullivan, or Paul and John; or DNA studies without Watson and Crick?

While we don't often think of them in an academic way, collaborations exist all around us. In fact, you've been collaborating most of your life in an informal fashion. How would you ever have finished that middle school science project without Mom or Dad (or both) spending all those hours offering advice and mixing papier-mâché for your inactive volcano? Or passed that algebra test without your best friend's quizzing over pizza and sodas?

And aren't those groups we played on such as the swim or basketball team really collaborations? And what about clubs like chess or debate? Let's not forget academics. Haven't your teachers placed you in groups to discuss research and present information on topics such as photosynthesis or did Shakespeare really write all those plays?

As you consider collaboration as a possible strategy to enhance your creative life, you need to ask and answer three important questions:

- Why collaborate?

- How do I establish a collaboration that works?

- What potential problems should I avoid?

What Is Applied Creative Thinking? / 45

Why Collaborate?

Perhaps the first question you'll want to answer is simply why collaborate? To have reached this stage in your education, you're probably done okay on your own, feeling a solitary satisfaction with that A on a paper or that award for an academic accomplishment. To collaborate is to surrender a bit of control as well as reward. You'll need something in return.

Try this list:

- **Increase your ideation levels.** Ideation is a fancy word for idea production, and research has consistently found that there's something to that old saying that two heads are better than one. Twenty five years ago initial studies found that collaboration increased ideation by 60-70%. Then a couple of years ago we read a business article that suggested that three or more collaborators could raise that rate to 400-700%. Small wonder that scientific research articles, which used to average four authors, now average 12!

- **Become more sociable.** In this digital age, isolation has become a serious issue. You may have seen the Sandra Bullock movie *The Net*, in which she plays a cyber-geek who has her identity stolen and cannot prove she is who she claims because nobody (work, bank, even fast-food restaurants) has ever seen her face-to-face. While you're probably no Bullockite (and, as we'll point out, many productive electronic collaborations exist), a face-to-face collaboration with an individual or group can become a positive, even nurturing experience.

- **Generate enthusiasm.** Have you ever watched a comedy on television or at the movies? Is your response the same if you're watching it alone as it is if you're with friends in your dorm room or in a crowded theater? Enthusiasm is contagious, and its energy can help a collaborative group through the long hours necessitated by a project.

- **Break down barriers.** Sometimes we all get caught up in our individual pursuits. Collaboration allows us to see beyond our special interests, to appreciate the interests of others. And isn't that what a liberal arts education is all about? Before your college days are finished, you'll probably realize that you learned almost as much from those collaborations you established (some in class, some outside) as you did from the formal curriculum. As we point out elsewhere, "the revised Bloom's pyramid has placed creating on top, but we as a university don't synthesize as well as we used to" (Blythe and Sweet, "Collaborating Your Scholarship" 69).

- **Sharpen understanding and communication skills.** When you work alone, you understand what you're doing; your intention is perfectly clear. The minute someone asks you what you're doing, you might encounter difficulty explaining your project. The very activity of explaining helps you clarify the process for yourself. In a collaborative setting the question/answer give-and-take sharpens all members' understanding. When they were younger, Charlie and Hal used to build decks and other structures as a get-away from the academic environment. While Charlie had the building expertise and was interested in getting the job done, one of Hal's major roles was to ask "the dumb question." Often Charlie was so engrossed in the project that he overlooked a potential problem until Hal's naive, "If we do that, won't…" made Charlie stop and reconsider the situation.

- **Use others' strengths to compensate for your weaknesses.** Just as in Hal and Charlie's building projects, collaborations offer you an opportunity to supplement your skills with those of others. In writing this book, Hal and Charlie brought 80-plus years of creativity to the table, but they were lacking in one extremely important area—technology. Rusty's expertise with current technology in the Noel Studio for Academic Creativity (not to mention his organizational skills) presented a perfect complement. You may be totally comfortable with the hands-on use of electronic devices, for instance, but need a collaborator to work on the presentation (either written or oral) of the findings of your project.

Could Toyota produce the most reliable car in the world if those "team members" didn't work together on the assembly line? Or Michael Phelps win his eighth gold medal at the 2008 Olympics without the combined efforts of his medley relay team? As we suggested above, collaborations don't even need to be face-to-face. For their last book of teaching tips for New Forums, Hal and Charlie collaborated electronically with colleagues from as far away as Australia. And even that collaboration seems "up close and personal" when we consider the distance between the NASA engineers and the astronauts who collaborated successfully to bring Apollo 13 home safely.

Forming Collaborations

Sometimes collaborations are forced upon us. Did any of you arrive on campus to meet for the first time that roommate with whom you would be spending a good amount of time during the semester? While you didn't choose this individual, you were going to have to "collaborate" in such matters as space, noise, and visitors in order to survive. Before the semester ends, you'll also probably encounter at least one class in which you'll become part of a group chosen by your instructor and required to work on a "group project" with these classmates regardless of compatibility.

While these forced collaborations are a fact of life, we want to focus on collaborations of choice, those you form as a strategy to enhance creativity. Perhaps a definition of collaboration will inform your choice. Vera John-Steiner, Robert Weber, and Michele Minnis claim:

> The principles in true collaboration represent complementary domains of expertise. They not only plan, decide, and act jointly, they also think together, combining independent conceptual schemes to create original framework. There is a commitment to shared resources, power, and talent; no individual's point of view dominates, authority for decisions and actions resides in the group, and work products reflect a blending of all participants' contributions. (776)

In order to establish a collaboration and make it work to enhance creativity, you should consider a few productive actions:

- **Find collaborators you respect.** You must believe in your collaborator's values and abilities. You have to trust the person's judgment and dependability.

- **Lose your ego.** Both Elvis and Frank Sinatra had a hit with a song titled "My Way." In a successful collaboration, there is no "my way," just "our way." By the time a project is complete, you shouldn't be able to recall which collaborator came up with which idea or direction. That element of respect again comes into play.

- **Establish roles early.** Since each collaborator has strengths, "the team must wisely divide the labor into the points each can perform effectively" (Blythe and Sweet, "Traits" 4). Use each member's strengths to assign tasks – researcher, writer, typist – but be willing to change roles if new ones emerge.

- **Establish attainable goals.** Never try to look only at the final goal; rather, set up a series of smaller goals (Research completed in three weeks, first draft of report by mid-term). When we began writing this book, the task seemed almost overwhelming, so we set up a schedule that allowed us to accomplish the project in smaller increments.

- **Be accountable for your part of the collaboration.** Never utter these accursed words, "I meant to." Your collaborators are counting on you; don't let them down.

- **Listen to what your collaborators say.** You may not agree with an idea initially, but, again, respect your collaborator enough to give that idea fair consideration. Often the give-and-take on an idea will produce other, more significant directions: "having someone else with an idea often stimulates something in the other" (Blythe and Sweet, "Collaborative Creativity" 9).

- **Take the time to reflect.** Periodically, step away from your project to view it from different angles; you might see an aspect you totally overlooked in the heat of creativity.

- **Keep good records.** Many brilliant ideas have been lost between inception and implementation because they were not recorded immediately. A written account of a session is also a good primer for the subsequent session.

Potential Problems

Will creative collaboration work for everyone? Probably not. Whether assigned or chosen, some collaborations never achieve success or even satisfaction. You may be an individual who simply works better alone—and you like it that way. You may be willing to give collaboration a try, but in your heart of hearts you know the process isn't for you. Even if collaboration sounds great to you, certain problems exist that you should consider.

- **Humans are basically competitive.** Sharing credit is difficult for some. All successful collaborations rest on mutual respect and loss of ego.

- **Those of like belief often don't make the best collaborators.** The famous poet William Blake claimed that "Without contraries is no progression." For this reason alone, you should choose collaborators who will question your ideas and cause you to consider other ways of approaching a problem. Carolyn Geer reports that "people learn best by collaborating with others who have radically different points of view" (R5).

- **Collaboration can lead to conflict.** Strong personalities often produce strong opinions. You must be willing to judge ideas and not those who produce them. The Beatles' infamous breakup was occasioned more by individual personalities (give Yoko a break) than by "creative differences."

- **Collaborators sometimes shirk responsibilities.** Life often intrudes on the best of intensions. Even with their collaborators depending on them, individuals will let the "tyranny of the urgent" stand in the way of their timely completion of a task.

- **Some collaborators find it difficult to communicate.** No collaboration can succeed without open lines of communication. All members of a collaboration must be kept "in the loop" as the project progresses. Timely reporting allows for periodic evaluation and adjustment.

Indeed, when used correctly, collaboration can be powerful toward enhancing your creativity. If two heads are better than one, think of what an entire group of collaborators can achieve.

Creative Concepts

- **Collaboration**—whether with one person or several—offers a powerful strategy for enhancing creativity.

- Collaborations depend on mutual respect between/among participants.

- Collaborations demand individual accountability.

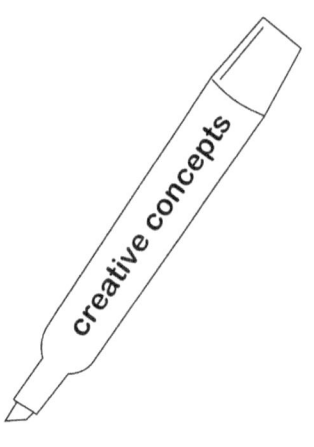

Exercises

1. Jot down a list of three traits you think characterize the ideal teacher (first date, best vacation). Then turn to the person on your right in class (who has also listed three) and negotiate until the two of you have arrived at a *collaborated* list of three. You might even expand the collaboration to include a pair of classmates across the table or in the seats in front of you. How did this collaboration change your initial lists? Why did some ideas remain and others disappear? How were the remaining ideas "better?" "Lesser?"

2. Break the class into groups of four or five. Give each group a pile of LEGO blocks and the tasks of building a structure. When the groups are finished, share the products. How are they similar? Different? Now have one member of each group move to another group with the task of "improving" the new group's structure. How is this member received?

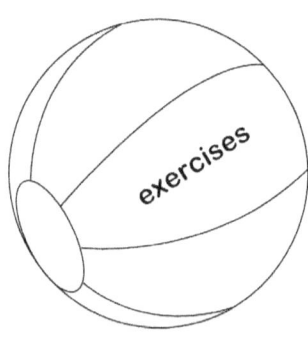

References

Blythe, Hal, and Charlie Sweet. "Collaborative Creativity." *It Works for Me, Creatively!* Eds. Hal Blythe and Charlie Sweet. Stillwater, OK: New Forums, 2011. 8-11. Print.

---. "Collabowriting Your Scholarship." *It Works for Me: Becoming a Publishing Scholar/Researcher*. Eds. Hal Blythe and Charlie Sweet. Stillwater, OK: New Forums, 2011. 67-73. Print.

---. "Traits for a Successful Collaboration." *It Works for Us, Collaboratively!* Eds. Hal Blythe and Charlie Sweet. Stillwater, OK: New Forums, 2011. 3-5. Print.

Geer, Carolyn T. "Innovation 101." *The Wall Street Journal* 17 Oct. 2011: R5. Print.

John-Steiner, Vera, Robert Weber, and Michele Minnis. "The Challenge of Studying Collaboration." *American Educational Research Journal* 35.4 (1998): 773–83. Print.

Sawyer, Keith. *Group Genius: The Creative Power of Collaboration*. New York: Basic Books, 2009. Print.

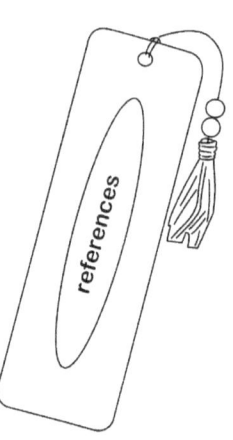

Basic Creative Strategies: Going with the Flow

Ever been told, "Just go with the flow?" Well, thanks to the work of Mihaly Csikszentmihalyi, going with the flow has a new meaning, and we'll bet it describes something old, something you've already experienced.

Ever play one of those near-perfect basketball games where you just couldn't seem to miss, the basket looked as big as a hula hoop, and you thought everybody else was moving in slow motion?

Ever been speeding along the highway so completely engrossed in a song on the radio that when it ends you can't figure out how you got so far down the road?

Ever done Internet research on something you cared about so passionately that you forgot to eat, attend class, or meet those friends you promised?

Ever play that piano piece or drum solo where every note sounded so loud, clear, and perfectly struck that you lost track of your environment?

Ever play a challenging videogame for so long you became lost in virtual space and when it was over, you not only had racked up record points but couldn't believe hours had passed since you started?

Sure you have, and afterwards, how did you explain the experience? "I was in the zone," "I was wired," "I was in the groove," or "I was one with it."

Back in the 19th century, William Wordsworth (surely the best name ever for a poet) wrote in *The Prelude* (1805 edition) about experiencing similar phenomena:

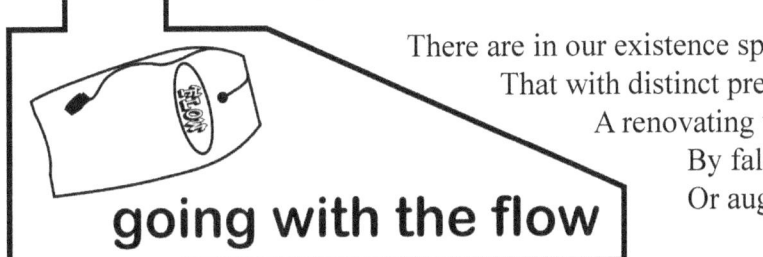

> There are in our existence spots of time,
> That with distinct pre-eminence retain
> A renovating virtue, whence–depressed
> By false opinion and contentious thought,
> Or aught of heavier or more deadly weight,
> In trivial occupations, and the round

>   Of ordinary intercourse–our minds
>   Are nourished and invisibly repaired;
>   A virtue, by which pleasure is enhanced,
>   That penetrates, enables us to mount,
>   When high, more high, and lifts us up when fallen. (12.208-218)

In these lines Wordsworth is describing moments similar to yours, but what he is ascribing to them is a therapeutic benefit—i.e., like sleep, they help repair and refresh our mind—but such moments also have another benefit. No matter the field, no matter when they occur, and no matter to whom, they allow for a fuller expression of creativity.

According to Csikszentmihalyi, the creator of the term, **Flow** produces his goal of happiness and is likewise healthy because of "the holistic experience that people feel when they act with total involvement" (36). In 1990 Csikszentmihalyi used as his subtitle for *Flow*, "The Psychology of Optimal Experience." In 1996 he offered this succinct definition: "The metaphor of 'flow' is one that many people have used to describe the sense of effortless action they feel in moments that stand out as the best in their lives" (29). And how do all these insight relate to creativity? According to Csikszentmihalyi, "Creativity involves the production of novelty. The process of discovery involved in creating something new appears to be one of the most enjoyable activities any human can be involved in" (*Creativity* 113).

So what conditions are necessary to produce the experience of flow? Csikszentmihalyi identifies nine elements that cut across all domains from athletics to art and religion to rock climbing.

1. **"clear goals every step of the way."** Higher-level sports provide that automatically as the goal is always to win. But for you in other endeavors the goals may be equally clear to you: achieve the highest level in that videogame, write an A paper, play that difficult piece perfectly, create an English sonnet, or solve the Saturday *New York Times* crossword puzzle.

2. **"immediate feedback to one's actions."** Maybe you start the ballgame with a "hot hand," you get to Level II faster than you ever have before and without mistakes, you write a paper introduction with a thesis that dazzles even you, you hear yourself striking all the proper keys, your first quatrain is perfect iambic pentameter with an ABBA rhyme scheme, and you finish the upper-left quadrant with no erasures or blank spaces.

3. **"a balance between challenges and skills."** Your defenders are good, but you are still getting your shots off and hitting over half of them; the paper's topic has stretched your research and writing skills, but you are able to say what you mean and say it well; you found writing free verse too easy, but admit that the sonnet structure is a worthy challenge; and while you can't finish the puzzle as fast as you can on easy Monday, you're not drawing a blank or leaving blank spaces.

4. **"Action and awareness are merged."** Your concentration is extremely intense.

5. **"Distractions are excluded from consciousness."** Not once in any of the endeavors has your mind digressed or your stomach summoned you.

6. **"no worry of failure."** As Ed Harris exclaimed in *Apollo 13*, "Failure is not an option." You are totally confident as you extend your fingers to release the ball, tap the keys, "tickle the ivories," pounce on the perfect rhyme, or fill in the next blank box.

7. **"Self-consciousness disappears."** You are the control freak in perfect control.

8. **"The sense of time becomes distorted."** Not only do you not look at your wrist or iPhone, but you are not aware of the concept of time.

9. **"The activity becomes an end in itself"** (*Creativity* 111-113). Whether you get win, get paid, or get published doesn't matter; only the sheer joy of the activity does.

Flow, then, is a goal and a self-assessing moment that demonstrates you have expressed your creativity.

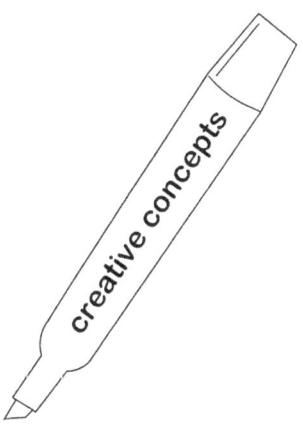

Creative Concepts

- Flow is a joyful moment.

- Flow is a refreshing moment.

- Flow is a moment of creativity.

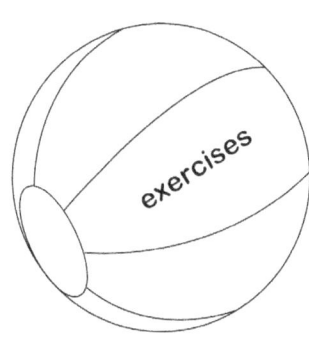

Exercises

1. Put yourself into a potential flow experience by choosing an activity you truly enjoy. Set up a specific, attainable, and challenging goal. When you start, begin with a part of your task that can give you an easy victory and focus only on the success of that goal. Try to block everything else out of your mind even if you conduct this experiment for only a few minutes.

2. When the experiment is over, rate yourself. Did you achieve the flow? Can you explain why? If you didn't, can you explain why not?

3. Make a list of some of your favorite moments of flow. If you can't think of a single instance of this phenomenon occurring to you, can you self-assess to figure out why it didn't?

References

Csikszentmihalyi, Mihaly. *Beyond Boredom and Anxiety*. San Francisco: Jossey-Bass, 1975. Print.

---. *Creativity*. New York: HarperCollins, 1996. Print.

---. *Flow: The Psychology of Optimal Experience*. New York: Harper & Row, 1990. Print.

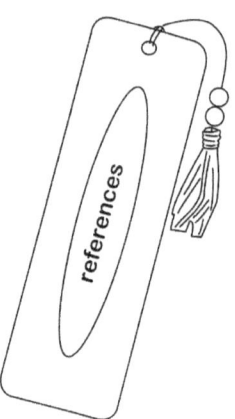

Basic Creative Strategies: Playing

A few days ago, Hal received an email from a boyhood friend containing shots of some vintage 1950's postcards with the caption, "These were the years that made me me." When Hal shared the email with Charlie, aside from feeling very old, they started thinking about the caption. What was it about those "growing-up" years that made such an impact—how had they made "me" me?

After kicking around the idea for a while, the Connecticut Yankee (Charlie) and the Kentucky son (Hal) realized that while they hailed from different backgrounds and parts of the county, their childhood experiences had one major aspect in common: **freedom**, a freedom that provided a spirit of adventure. As boys they had awakened every morning convinced that, in the words of the poet John Milton, "the world was all before them" (*Paradise Lost*, XII, 1.646); they were free to "create" it as they wished. Whether it was playing a pick-up ballgame in the vacant lot down the street or building the new Fort Apache in the neighbor's woods, they could be Ted Williams socking another homerun, or the gallant Lt. Masters firing his carbine at the approaching hostiles. Their only limit was nightfall, or Mom's yelling, "Supper!"

During those middle school years, however, things started to change. Sure, girls came along, but it was more than that. Choose-sides ballgames became tryouts for the school team, then the keep-score games; rusty-nailed plank forts became shop-assigned jewelry boxes…and somewhere along the line, most of the fun disappeared.

High school, college, and grad school brought more of the same. Amidst the continuum of school, work, part-time jobs, studying for SATs or GREs, and sending out resumes, these once-upon-a-time kids almost forgot what it was like to experience that spirit of adventure, to shape their world. They were so intent on playing by the rules that they were letting the rules play them.

Then something strange happened that changed everything. During their first years at Eastern Kentucky University they were assigned as office-mates. Both college athletes, they decided to give tennis a try as a doubles team (this was during the 1970s tennis boom). Their conversations in the office and on the court, along with the University's purchase of some state-of-the-art television equipment, led to their forming a collaboration in everything from movie scripts to mystery stories, not to mention more than a few scholarly (but hopefully never dull) articles.

Why this lengthy story? What could the chronicle of the lives of two egg-head professors possibly contribute to a book on creativity?

Glad you asked! Shortly after Hal and Charlie started writing together, they penned (that was in those ancient days before the computer) a fantasy story that might answer your questions. In the story, the protagonist, a young, up-and-coming businessman, was troubled nightly by a dream in which he saw himself as a boy playing in a makeshift fort in the woods. As the dream unfolded, the boy became fearful of a shadowy figure lurking in the trees outside the fort. Every morning the man donned his corporate-approved blue polyester suit (hey, it was the 1970s), wolfed down his breakfast as he argued with his wife about this or that, then headed for the job he hated even though it brought him lots of prestige and money. The dream continued to grow more vivid as the man's struggles to hold his world together became more futile. One night after a shouting match with his boss and a conversationless dinner with his wife, the dream seemed almost real. As the shadow figure advanced toward the fort, the boy raised his Red Ryder BB gun and fired. The figure fell in the tall grass. When the boy approached the motionless man, he recognized the blue suited figure was his adult self.

The story's point? The dream revealed that the man had allowed his drive for success to turn him into a monster of sorts, a thing that would have been scary for him as a boy. William Wordsworth, another of those famous writers we're always quoting, said, "The child is father of the man" ("My Heart Leaps Up"). What he meant was that as we grow older, our lives dull the spark that we possess as children, and our natural creativity is extinguished by the rules and structures that society places on us. Interestingly, a few years ago, Kenneth Koch confirmed Wordsworth's claim when he conducted a study with inner-city children. The study revealed that kids who had remarkable creative abilities (demonstrated through poetry) started to lose their creativity as they matured. By the time they were ready to enter middle school, creativity was greatly diminished.

That drain on natural creativity was exactly what Charlie and Hal's fateful collaboration saved them from enduring. Over the years their office has become somewhat of a museum of pop culture, filled with movie posters, bobbleheads, and comic books. And every morning they arrive at their own "green room" to prepare for the day with the same spirit of adventure that they enjoyed as children.

Stuart Brown and Christopher Vaughan, who do workshops for corporations on improving employee innovation by understanding play, claim rightly that "play is a state of mind, rather than an activity" (60). And they are careful to point out that "play and work are mutually supportive. They are not poles at opposite ends of our world" (121). As Hal and Charlie have discovered, many of their most creative efforts have arisen from those free-wheeling times spent in the office, smashing round ideas like tennis balls. Teresa Amabile, et. al. capture the nature of their exchanges when they claim, "It's as if the mind is throwing a bunch of balls into the creative spread, juggling them around until they collide in interesting ways" (53). Those "interesting ways" have led to many publications and loads of fun. But more importantly for their sanity, these playful moments have allowed them to, as Patricia Ryan Madson puts it, "reconnect with our own creative force, to see the world in color again…to shake loose rigid patterns of thinking and doing" (19).

What is this thing we call **PLAY**? You probably have at least a foggy notion, but have you ever really thought about what goes into this vital component of life? Again, Madson is informative as she lists a few essential traits:

- Apparently purposeless—it is done for its own sake;

- Voluntary—it is not obligatory or required by duty;

- Inherent attraction—it's fun; it makes you feel good;

- Freedom from time—we lose a sense of the passing of time;

- Diminished consciousness of self—we stop worrying about whether we look good or awkward, smart or stupid; we are fully in the moment, what is called "**flow**";

- Improvisional potential—we are open to serendipity, to chance; and,

- Continuation desire—we desire to keep doing it. (67-68)

Insightfully, Madson claims that play is <u>apparently</u> purposeless. Charlie and Hal, along with anyone who has ever experienced the results of allowing that playful state of mind to hold sway, will attest to a strong relationship between play and productivity; as Brown and Vaughan put it, "Play is the mother of invention" (135).

Pat Kane, one of the foremost theorists in the play ethic, makes a strong case for the world of work's need for play in order to reach its potential.

- Play helps release thoughts that are locked in the head and heart.

- You see things differently. Ideas come to life with more concrete detail than ideas expressed through just talking.

- Discussion during play happens on a more level playing field.

- The group at play thrives only when everybody participates, so frustrations are reduced, and team coherence and direction is more solid.

- Play tests your experiment, to explore and take risks with ideas without fearing consequences that might happen "in real life."

- You generate a wider and more imaginative range of possibilities during play than you would during a traditional business meeting.

- People at play are more present, more engaged, more passionate and better performers. (84-85)

Unfortunately, our current culture, especially our educational system, seems intent on destroying, or at least diminishing, the potential power of play. All those forces that initially dulled Charlie and Hal's spirit of adventure have assumed an ever more powerful position today. Nowadays, parents transport kids from one adult-organized-and-run activity (music, sports, art) to the next, and schools insist on an archaic rote-information approach to learning, while at the same time eliminating "nonessential" subjects such as art, music, physical education—and even recess.

Such forward thinkers as David Pink and Erica McWilliam have demonstrated the harm of these well-meaning actions in light of the need to develop graduates equipped to fill jobs calling for more creativity and initiative than those of yesterday. Brown and Vaughan echo with:

> The advantages that countries like the United States…retain is the ability to invent—to dream up solutions to problems that people may not yet even know they have. Notions that remain economically strong are those that can create intellectual property—and the ability to innovate largely comes out of an ability to play. (200)

Kane goes so far as to claim that "Play will be to the 21st century what work has been to the past three hundred years."

The spirit of adventure, that playful state of mind, served us well as children. And even though we didn't realize it then—or even care—the games and fantasies of those early years were a type of practice for later life. Our "do overs" and arguments on the sandlot ball field were preparing us for more complex and important negotiations as adults; our crudely built forts were forerunners of shiny skyscrapers during a career in architecture.

Brown and Vaughan conclude one of their chapters with a brief but powerful statement: "When we stop playing, we start dying" (73). After completing this chapter, Charlie and Hal ran through those old postcards again, this time with even more joy than the first time, since they realized that "what made me me"—that ability to play—was still alive and kicking.

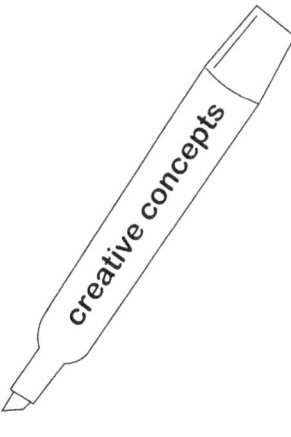

Creative Concepts

- **Play** is a state of mind that kindles our openness to the world around us.

- Play is not the opposite of work, but a mutually supportive complement.

- The future will belong to the creative, and playfulness fosters creativity.

- Childhood play provides practice for adult situations.

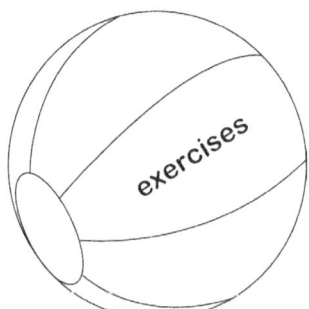

Exercises

1. Divide the class into several groups of four or five. Have one member of each group choose an object from a backpack or purse and immediately give one possible use for the object. Then have each member of the group come up with another use—no matter how seemingly strange—until you run out of uses. How long could you go?

2. Divide the class into groups of four or five. Have each member of the group make a list of five strange things about him/herself, one of which is not true. See if the other members of the group can spot the fib.

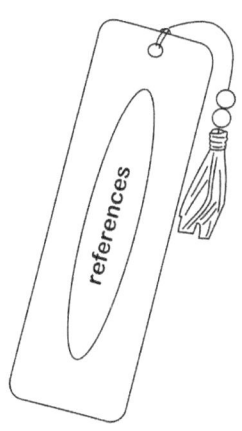

References

Amabile, Teresa, Constane Hadley, and Steven Kramer. "Creativity Under the Gun." *Harvard Business Review* 80.8 (2002): 52-61. Print.

Brown, Stuart, and Christopher Vaughan. *Play: How It Shapes the Brain, Opens the Imagination, and Invigorates the Soul*. New York: Penguin, 2010. Print.

Kane, Pat. *The Play Ethic: A Manifesto for a Different Way of Living*. London: Pan Books, 2005. Print.

Kock, Kenneth. *Wishes, Lies, and Dreams*. New York: HarperCollins, 1980. Print.

Madson, Patricia. *Improv Wisdom: Don't Prepare, Just Show Up*. New York: Bell Tower, 2005. Print.

McWilliam, Erica. *The Creative Workforce*. Sydney: UNSW Press, 2008. Print.

Pink, Daniel. *A Whole New Mind: Why Right-Brainers Will Rule the Future*. New York: Penguin, 2005. Print.

Basic Creative Strategies: Recognizing Pattern

Pssst! Wanna know a secret?

Of course you do, but what if we told you we're about to let you in on the secret of all secrets? The great meta-secret of all disciplines?

Here it is then. Every domain from arts to sports, business to science, Hollywood to HGTV, and quilting to kite-making has at its core one or more patterns. By patterns, we mean a repetition of similar motifs and ideas. Essentially our brains automatically record all sense impressions and sort them into categories. Familiar faces can be separated into friends and non-friends, music into classical, children's, pop, country, and whatever. Sometimes we create these patterns consciously, and sometimes our brains function on auto-pilot. Sometimes over time we can learn patterns, such as "How To Pick Up a Guy in a Non-Bar Situation" or "How to Hit a Fast-Pitched Softball."

Are you the kind of person who enjoys connecting the adult dots, looking for connections between things, or even trying to offer different solutions to the challenges presented on HGTV's *All American Handyman*?

Acting upon pattern recognition can make you successful in your chosen field. All-time Major League home-run hitter, Hank Aaron, for example, attributed his ability to go deep to grasping and applying this concept. He claimed that every time he faced a pitcher, his mind took pictures of the ball coming toward him, and he filed them in his brain under categories like curve ball, change-up, and forkball. After a while, every time he saw a pitch, he knew almost instantly which type it was and what it would do; comparing it to his mental catalogue and coupled with his superb reactions, he was able to adjust to the ball's speed and movement in order to hit it out of the park.

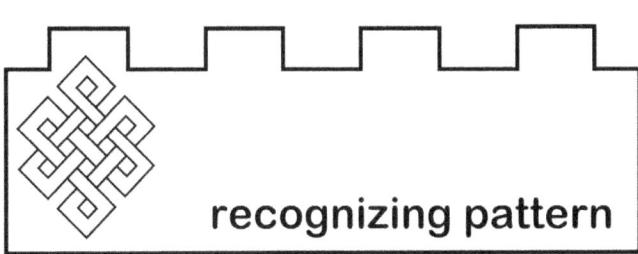

One academic field you may not have heard of, comparative mythology, involves analyzing mythologies from the Hebrew to the Norse and from the American Indian to the Asian Indian in order to discover insights and similarities. Back in 1949 Joseph Campbell published a breakthrough book called *The Hero with a Thousand Faces*. In it he discovered that most of the world's myths could be boiled down to an essential "monomyth" wherein each hero underwent a pattern of separation-initiation-return. His insight influenced thousands of artists, but the one work with which you are probably most familiar is the *Star Wars* saga. George Lucas even admitted that his initiation story of Luke Skywalker's maturation into a Jedi Knight would have been impossible had he not read and employed Campbell's seminal work as the underlying pattern to his space opera.

Pattern Recognition is the ability to discern what American novelist Henry James called the "figure in the carpet"—hitherto unperceived threads that weave through the tapestry of one or more domains. While the term is often used in machine learning, we are using it in a larger context.

For instance, Hal and Charlie have always loved graphic novels and remember fondly when the four-color fantasies were mere "comic books" that were thought in their childhoods to seduce the innocent and cause juvenile delinquency. In the early 80s, as pop culture became a legitimate academic domain and the subject of college courses across the nation, they began to wonder if stupendous superhero stories (comic books once thrived on alliteration) in the DC and Marvel Universes subscribed to Campbell-like theories. In fact, another pop culture theorist named John Cawelti in books such as *The Six-Gun Mystique* demonstrated that westerns, romances, and mysteries followed basic "conventions" or patterns of character, plot development, and theme. Charlie and Hal pored through their collection of comic books (what a great excuse to reread these classics), and by applying Cawelti and Campbell to a new field, they ended up publishing an article in *The Comics Journal* that demonstrated how superhero sagas did indeed follow a six-step progression of conventions.

Pattern recognition usually begins in observation. Newton recognized a design in the simple act of an apple dropping from a tree. Archimedes saw the principle of buoyancy and displacement in a bathtub. Sonar derived from the observation of dolphins and bats, and even the outdoor amphitheater owes its shape to the ear.

Pattern recognition progresses past a mere noticing of something to include what preceded the thing noticed and what followed it—i.e., it discerns a linked chain of things. Maybe you're just fooling around with your guitar or piano, and you hear something you like. It's not one note or a chord (three notes played simultaneously), but part of a larger unit. After many iTunes downloads, you begin to grasp a pattern, the so-called "three chord trick"—that is, that by mastering just three chords, you could play thousands of pop rock classics. Have you ever listened over and over to a CD in which members of a group wrote all the songs and thought that the songs started to sound alike? That's probably because the songwriters found a pattern they liked and stuck with it with only minor variations.

How do you learn to recognize patterns in pop and academia? Notice in the previous example you were listening to music "over and over." Do you think you would recognize a familiar pattern in Hemingway if you read just "The Short Happy Life of Francis Macomber?" Suppose you perused not only Papa's short stories, but his novels, too. Obviously once again **expertise** plays a major role. Now, what if you read not only Hemingway's essays describing his own literary theories but also essays on them by literary critics? Do you think it would easier to detect Hemingway's use of existentialism or his iceberg theory? In short, the more familiar you are with a subject, the easier it is to recognize patterns. Another way to state this idea is that long-term **experience** and **deliberate practice** will help you to recognize these patterns.

But there's a "trick" that can sometimes shortcut pattern recognition. In a previous example we discussed applying theories from the field of comparative mythology to pop culture studies, and we also showed you how direct observation of nature can be utilized in other fields (botany and clothing manufacture collide in the discovery of Velcro). Practice "crossing over." For instance, one variation of Ohm's Law states that electricity follows the path of least resistance. Could that law be applied to human behavior? Do human beings tend to follow pathways of least resistance? Is there a psychological equivalent to science's Doppler Effect?

Creative processes work the same way. Brainstorming in psychology might help you brainstorm in your Art 101 class. A polymath is a term for people like Leonardo da Vinci, who are very good at a variety of subjects. One explanation for such people is they are born geniuses, but another is that they developed an understanding of creative processes that they could then apply to a variety of fields.

Now a caveat. Pattern Recognition is a good skill to learn and practice, but don't overdo it. **Apophenia** is our tendency to see patterns where there are none. How many theories have suggested that President John Kennedy was not shot by a lone gunman? Conspiracy theory, whether it's about moon-landings or UFOs, often goes off on unproveable tangents. A show called *Sasquatch Hunters* ("Ah, the game's bigfoot") might draw respectable cable ratings, but we don't yet have a yeti corpse to study. In truth, your creative mind will look for patterns, but it's up to your critical thinking side to verify these patterns.

One more caveat. As with other creative strategies, the more motivated you are and the more you are interested in searching for patterns, the better at it you'll be.

Creative Concepts

- **Pattern Recognition** is the ability to discern the figure in the carpet by weaving together separate strands into a coherent whole.

- Pattern Recognition begins with observation and is enhanced by expertise, experience, and deliberate practice.

- Pattern Recognition must be verified by critical thinking so as to avoid **apophenia**.

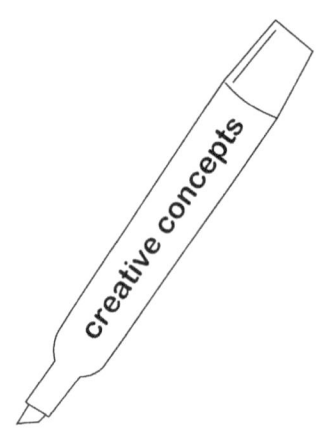

Exercises

1. Choose a field in which you have some expertise and experience. Search for a pattern. For instance, if you enjoy playing basketball, check out some footage of great jump-shooters. What do you notice about where their hands are when they catch a pass? Where do their eyes go next, to the person guarding them or toward the hoop? What's the minimum height needed to shoot a three-point J? What is the angle of the arc? Where does the elbow point? How does the shooter's hand finish up? A pattern exists, and if no one has yet taught it to you, you can still pick it up and apply it to better your game.

2. Pick an easy crossword puzzle (if you do the *New York Times* puzzle, try Monday or Tuesday). As you solve the puzzle, set up a simple notation system for cataloguing the clues. You are not only going to fill in the Acrosses and Downs, but you are going to look for patterns in the types of clues. For instance, you might use F=Facts (e.g., Lawrence of Arabia in Hollywood), D=Definitions (e.g., Collect), P=Puns (e.g., Mass appeal, where Mass is the religious ritual), O=Obscure terms (e.g., synectics), and even C=Canon (for words/concepts/facts you must know—e.g., ort, E-I-E-I-O, Earp), T=Themes (e.g., comic movies). Some of the labels will overlap. If you were to try this experiment for an entire week, which types of answers do you think would predominate on Monday and Tuesday? What do you think would happen by Saturday and Sunday? The answer is obviously a pattern, but what kind?

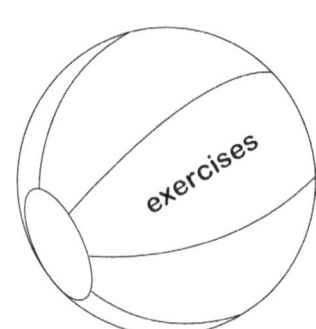

References

Blythe, Hal, and Charlie Sweet. "Formula and the Superhero." *The Comics Journal* 73 (July 1982): 82-88. Print.

Campbell, Joseph. *The Hero with a Thousand Faces*. Princeton: Princeton University Press, 1968. Print.

Cawelti, John. *The Six-Gun Mystique*. Bowling Green, OH: Bowling Green State University, 1984. Print.

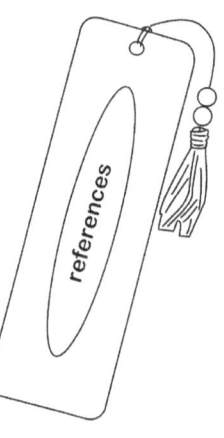

Basic Creative Strategies: Using Metaphor

In *Learning to Think Things Through*, Gerry Nosich provides a four-step process for people to see if they understand a concept, usually a new one, called S-E-E-I:

1. State it

2. Elaborate (explain it more fully, in your own words)

3. Exemplify (give a good example)

4. Illustrate.

Often, Nosich explains, "your illustration will be a picture in words, an analogy, simile, or metaphor that captures the meaning" (24-25). Nosich's fourth step not only clarifies your understanding of a concept, but in another sense it creates meaning.

Metaphor, then, is an effective creative strategy.

Most people think of metaphor as a decorative device reserved for poets, something you learn about in your classes and then forget. Somewhere in your memory is a statement like a metaphor is a comparison wherein one object is likened to another and given its traits. The key to a metaphor is not to take it too literally. When Paul Simon sings, "I am a rock," he is not saying that he is a solid aggregate of minerals, but simply he has chosen that self-image because "a rock feels no pain."

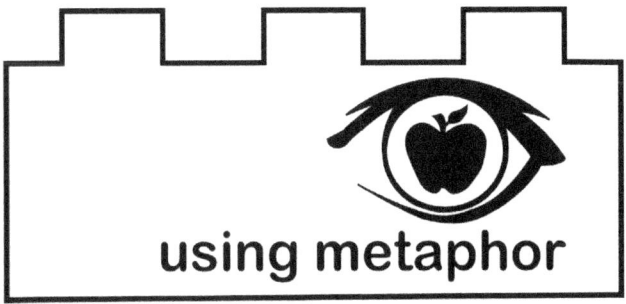

In fact, coming up with a metaphoric representation of something helps you learn it in a creative way. In *Borrowing Brilliance* David Kord Murray even claims that "a creative idea begins either consciously or subconsciously, with a metaphor or analogy. By using a metaphor, a comparison of one thing with another, you intellectually connect the two things. Once this connection is made, the metaphor is extended and the two things are allowed to grow, merging the two ideas together" (110). Appropriately, the word metaphor derives from a Greek word meaning "transfer."

If a metaphor can be a strategy for creativity, knowing how a metaphor works is obviously quite important. Every metaphor can be separated into two parts. The first part, the **tenor,** is the subject, often abstract, of the comparison, and the **vehicle** is the object or more concrete way in which the tenor is described (or as the old song says, "I'm your vehicle, baby. I'll take you anywhere you want to go"). Apple recently employed a series of commercials involving two actors, one representing the Apple computer named Mac and one representing the rivals called PC, that makes the metaphoric process obvious. The actors were the concrete vehicles representing the objects, the opposing computers. PC was older and dressed in a suit to suggest that PCs are aimed at more formal business persons, while Mac was younger and wore sports clothes, suggesting Mac is the computer for youthful, fun-loving, less stodgy folks.

Some commercials use metaphor less obviously. If you are told that the new Volvo Valentino "embraces" the road, you realize that the implied comparison is of an automobile to a lover. But by using that comparison, the metaphor is leading you to think of other ways that comparison might be true: does it try to "please" you? What is its touch like?

Hemingway once said that "The dignity of movement of an ice-berg is due to only one-eighth of it being above the water" (192). Good metaphors are creative because they force us to go beneath the surface, to look deeper for things not so obvious. When writers use metaphors, they want us to probe beyond the obvious, and they want us to search for meaning rather than telling us exactly what to think.

So, do all metaphors force us to probe beneath the surface? Actually those in two extremes don't. On one hand, a metaphor can be a simple cliché such as "Your mind is in the gutter." Cliched metaphors are STOP signs for our mind. Because we've heard them so often, our minds shut down. At the other extreme, some metaphors can be too complicated to comprehend, such as "Eleanor embodied Newton's laws of motion." OK, which laws of motion? Was she always in motion? Mainly at a stand-still?

Metaphors not only probe beneath the surface, but like unmanned submarines with cameras they allow us to see things at great depths. In Shakespeare's *A Midsummer's Night Dream*, Theseus says,

> And as imagination bodies forth
> The forms of things unknown, the poet's pen
> Turns them to shapes and gives to airy nothing
> A local habitation and a name. (Act V, Scene 1, ll. 14-17)

Paradoxically, what the Bard of Avon is saying is that we often see things more clearly at a distance—i.e., the metaphor offers us a perspective.

Remember a TV show that ran from 1997-2003, *Buffy the Vampire Slayer*? In the long tradition of vampire lore Angel was a metaphor for the taboo nature of sexuality for young teenagers. Providing a key insight, Joss Whedon, the show's creator, claims that the entire series revolved around a central metaphor, "high school as horror show." In fact, Jane Espenson explained that every script for the show started with a deliberate choice of some type of teenage angst from acne to loneliness. Then a monster or demon was created to become the metaphor for that problem. At the end of the hour, Buffy would vanquish the demon and more importantly the angst issue in a celebration of feminine power. The monster-of-the-week metaphor allowed the show to deal with sensitive issues from a distance that created an emotional bond as well as a new understanding in its audience. Note how as Buffy matured as a person, her solutions evolved from slaying, to befriending, and even trysting with the "enemy." The monster was the "local habitation and a name" that allowed Buffy to confront the tribulations of teenagerdom.

Is metaphor alive and kicking (to use a metaphor)? On the day we write this piece (11 September 2011), the Review section (C) of *The Wall Street Journal* contains a column that defines a screenplay as "a story in the shape of a prayer" (C12), an article that describes George Preston Marshall (the owner of the Washington Redskins) as "a tragic figure" (C9), a book review that finds the circus a common metaphor for romance (C8), and Penn Gillette comparing modern politics to a Vegas magic act (C3). All four vehicles help elucidate their tenors.

Creative Concepts

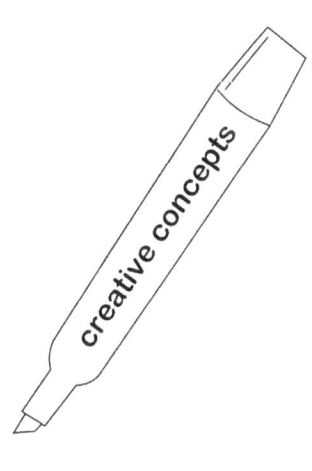

- **Metaphor** is an effective creative strategy for learning about the unknown and gaining a perspective on it.

- Metaphors have two components, a **tenor** (the actual subject, often abstract/emotional) and a **vehicle** (the familiar image or object used to help make the subject known).

- Effective metaphors avoid the extremes of clichés and excessive complexity.

- Metaphors provide perspective and allow the exploration of shadowy dimensions of the mind and emotions.

Exercises

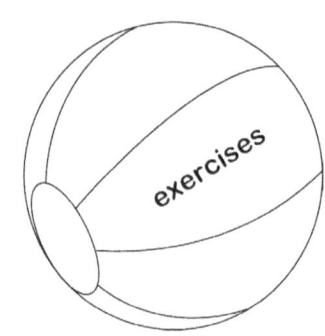

1. Pretend you are in the writers' room with Josh and Jane. First, select a problematic emotion or idea with which you have grappled. Second, embody that emotion/idea as a monster or demon. Third, compose a short narrative in which you confront the monster/demon. Fourth, craft an ending to your narrative. Do you see yourself or your main protagonist defeating said monster/demon, fighting it to a draw, befriending it, or succumbing to it?

2. An easy way to construct a metaphor is to create a simile, which is a comparison using "like" or "as." Try composing your own simile by completing some of the following:

   - My parents treat me like a _____.

   - My best friend is as _____ as a _____.

   - The most powerful emotion hit me like a _____.

   - Trying to understand _____ is like _____.

3. Try to avoid trite metaphors that have become clichés. Look at your fill-ins for the previous four. Did the cliché-meter register 10 because that powerful emotion hit you like a brick, a sledgehammer, or a run-away train?

References

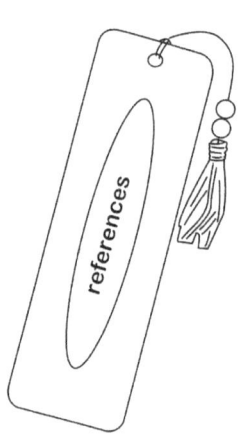

"Buffy the Vampire Slayer (TV series)." *Wikipedia*. n.d. Web. 12 Sept. 2011.

Hemingway, Ernest. *Death in the Afternoon*. New York: Scribner's, 1932. Print.

"Life and Culture: Review Section." *The Wall Street Journal* 11 Sept. 2012. Print.

Murray, David Kord. *Borrowing Brilliance*. New York: Gotham Books, 2009. Print.

Nosich, Gerald. *Learning to Think Things Through*. Upper Saddle River, NJ: Prentice Hall, 2006. Print.

The Creative Thinking Environment

Let's face it, creativity looks unproductive. It doesn't look like work or school in any traditional sense. What does it look like? It might look like play, talking, or something even more abstract. Creativity might look visual—it can come in the form of maps, outlines, and drawings. Creativity can also look like you're making things with your hands or with technology. You might have blocks or LEGOs in a common area—the stuff of creativity, as Sir Ken Robinson might say. If you're more technologically sophisticated, you might choose touch-screen technologies over other alternatives. The question is, though, how do we foster that creative environment? All these resources don't mean a thing if you're not cultivating intentional creative thinking - that is, creating time and space for it to occur.

Let's back up a bit. Creative thinking should be intentional, and your environment must cultivate intellectual time and space for creative thinking to occur. But what does that really mean? Well, at first sight, it might mean creating time for contemplation. For students, this might mean time for collaboration around a problem or issue. For employees, it might mean time to employ **divergent thinking** or free time to consider problems and design possible solutions. Employees might have 24 hours to leave their traditional work environment to develop a new product, concept, or pitch. They **converge** after that free period and pitch their concept to their peers or supervisors. The point? Allow time for creativity—open-ended sessions for considering problems from many perspectives; that time for generating ideas is time well spent. Take time to ask questions. "If you were an employer, which portfolio would you prefer?" "Which design would make you more likely to buy a product?"

Creativity necessarily involves time for **generative thinking**. Does that mean generating ideas without a goal? No! Generative thinking usually involves an objective. But what does generative thinking entail?

- Free-form thinking

- Associative thinking

- Concept development
- Risk taking
- Experimentation

Leaders must model creative environments. You can't just talk about creativity. Creative thinking must permeate all aspects of your environment—from physical space design to the structure of meetings. We can't overlook space design, though. What are the elements of a creative space?

- Color
- Flow
- Spontaneous collaboration
- High-touch

Let's first explore the role of color in the creative environment. It might seem simple, and it won't make up for a lack of intellectual space for creativity to prosper, but it can go a long way toward inviting people to share their ideas openly—creating an inviting space for conversation. Colors create an energy that can lead to creative innovation. When one is considering the design of space, colors can come in the form of objects or manipulatives. Or, color can come in the design of furniture or art. Students and employees can provide their own forms of artistic expression; some of the most beautiful designs are intellectual or abstract. Instead of painting the walls white, perhaps paint them with dry-erase paint, like ideapaint (http://www.ideapaint.com/). Color within the space can create an energy that yields creative ideas and concepts and challenges unproductive standards, including stagnant meetings and lackluster concepts.

Flow can also enhance the creative environment. It can come in the form of people and ideas.

- Where do people do their best work?
- Where do people congregate?
- Are there common areas that could turn into creative areas?
- Does the environment invite spontaneous collaboration?
- Does the environment invite people to share ideas? Moreover, can they express ideas visually, publically?
- How do people work out problems? By thinking quietly and independently in a cubicle?

Independent work might have its time and place in the creative environment, but it doesn't provide opportunities for rapid-fire thinking and exploration of a variety of concepts. The creative environment invites the casual passerby into the conversation—knowing that there's much to gain from casual comment and the free-flow of ideas. An environment with creative flow invites **serendipitous** interaction. It's high-touch; that is, it takes control out of the communicator's hands and puts responsibility on the audience as well. It encourages leaders as well as participants to interact with concepts. High-touch concepts promote high-energy environments. The design of a creative environment must consider the flow of spaces. Space design must be conducive to sharing ideas, which will often mean bringing them into a public realm.

The creative environment invites participation. All ideas are good ideas to start. Writing spaces come off the page to the table, wall, screen, and common space where minds meet. Let those ideas grow and develop, invite divergent thinking, and encourage participation from a variety of people and sources. We always like to associate different points and concepts just to see what the outcome might look like. Put those ideas side-by-side—physically move ideas around with writable tiles or Post-it notes.

Vera John-Steiner suggests in *Creative Collaboration* that integrative collaboration facilitates transformative change. Creative environments will facilitate these ongoing, sustained collaborative efforts. Integrative collaborative efforts create space that involves students, for example, working side-by-side and in concert with instructors. The creative environment does not divide people but facilitates an environment where ideas are respected and given ample consideration, where some of the most far-fetched possibilities have merit. Integrative collaboration can yield tangible results, too. Musical composers, artists, and authors all benefit from creative environments.

The most creative environments have dimension. That is, they are not one-dimensional. They include visual, auditory, and, especially given developments in technology, kinesthetic qualities. Music can trigger the memory and inspire a thought that was not present beforehand. In a way, music adds a deeper dimension to the creative environment. Creative environments engage different learning styles. Auditory learning will respond well to music or oral communication, while some will work best by doing. Interactive technologies allow for hands-on creators to build ideas, physically making meaning and with their hands through high or low tech products.

At some point in your career, probably in the near future, you're going to be asked to produce a text that doesn't exist on the traditional printed page. You might ask, now, how and why? In particular, industry demands on college graduates are pushing the boundaries of technology. What if your employer asks you to create a digital promotional video? Where would you start?

Our guess is that you need a writable space. What if you had a full wall without borders or barriers to your thinking? Your end product is necessarily visual; it's a video. It also involves aural communication, right? Sound, perhaps music. What about oral communication? Are you going to set the video to a voiceover? What if you've never produced a multimodal product before? What kind of environment would you want? Back to that "writable" space, again. You're going to need somewhere to grow your ideas; say, a **Greenhouse**. In the **Noel Studio for Academic Creativity**, we've included a bright, open space with multiple skylights where ideas are free to come to life (for a longer description of creative environments, see Ezarik). It's full of sights and sounds, where artifacts bounce off the page; where you can move and interact with just about everything—from the furniture to the technology.

Perhaps most importantly, though, you can make the environment your own. We're at our best when we're comfortable, right? Yes! So, you're comfortable when you can adapt your environment to the task, problem, or project at hand, then. We need intellectual space to invent ideas, right? Free time to think and create. What would an environment conducive to invention look like? Colorful, open, comfortable seating? Yes, that's your perfect **invention space**. In traditional spaces, you seize any little corner you can. In a creative environment, every little corner becomes your canvas. Creative thinking isn't best taught in a lecture hall or from behind a podium. You learn by doing, right? By focusing on collaboration, as you might have guessed, the space engages you. The goal for the Noel Studio's creative environment is to **immerse** you in the creative process—the space is yours to treat as your creative canvas. We're compelled when we feel consumed by creativity—the feeling of being submerged in bright color and energy that you just can't find anywhere else. Here's where you're at your best. The problem is to develop an innovative video clip. Well, let's spread out the butcher paper and **storyboard** our concept. You just can't immerse yourself in creative thinking if you're constrained by rows or bolted chairs. Just as creative thinking will take you off the traditional page, the creative environment will take you out of your chair, putting in your hands the tools and resources of creative thinking. The teacher is no longer there to tell you, step-by-step, what to do. It's your turn to create and **innovate**. The creative environment prompts YOU to take the lead. Are you going to sit in the corner, or are you going to take charge of your creative environment?

Creative Concepts

- A **Creative Thinking Environment** must cultivate intellectual <u>time</u> and <u>space</u> for such thinking to occur.

- Generative Thinking involves an objective/goal.

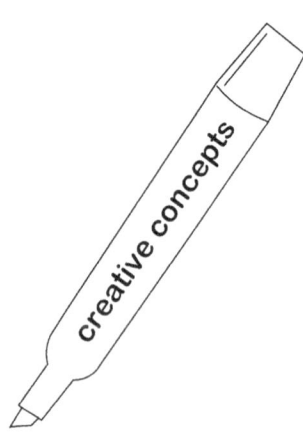

- A Creative Thinking Environment invites casual comments and the free flow of ideas.

- A Creative Thinking Environment engages different learning styles.

- A Creative Thinking Environment encourages freedom.

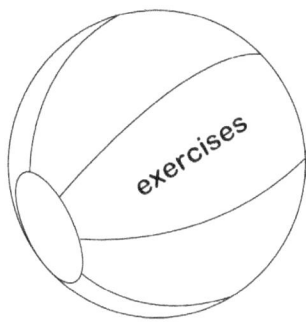

Exercises

1. Look at the arrangement of your classroom. If you could rearrange the furniture and equipment in any fashion, what would you do? Why?

2. Have the class divided into groups of four or five. Assign each group the task of designing the ideal creative thinking environment, including lighting, color, temperature and technology. Each group must choose a manner by which they will present their design to the class.

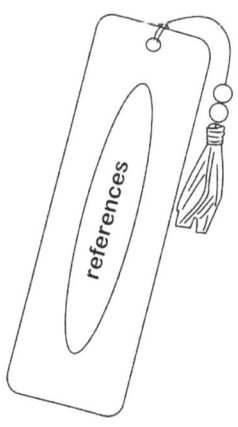

References

Ezarik, Melissa. "Collaboration Station." *University Business: Solutions for Higher Education Management* 14.5 (2011): 36-41. EBSCOhost. Web. 12 Oct. 2011.

Ideapaint. N.d. 14 Sept. 2011. <http://www.ideapaint.com/>.

John-Steiner, Vera. *Creative Collaboration.* New York: Oxford University Press, 2000. Print.

Assessing Creative Thinking from Many Angles

Just as a distinction is made between "Big C" and "little c" creativity, perhaps we should claim a difference between Big Assessment and little assessment. **Big C assessment** is formal (often called psychometrics), has a test specifically designed for an objective, and is performed by experts attempting to measure one of the **Four Ps—the creative person, process, product, and press**. **"Little c" assessment**, on the other hand, is informal, has no specified test, and is undertaken by the would-be creators in order to render a judgment on their ideas, their processes, their products, and/or their environments. Testing concepts such as reliability and validity are applied to the former, whereas self-assessments are less precise and vary from person to person, often depending on the field. For the most part, unless you are going into testing-specific fields (e.g., statistics, psychology), or perhaps you were diagnosed/not diagnosed as gifted, you probably have little interest in formal assessment measures, so this chapter will summarize the former, but emphasize "little c" assessment.

Experts appear to agree that no perfect test for "Big C" creativity exists, and perhaps one reason is that no one definition of creativity is accepted. To examine creativity at all, test creators must first offer a precise definition of how they view creativity. To emphasize this point, Jonathan Plucker, Ronald Beghetto, and Gayle Dow argue creativity is "the interaction among *aptitude*, *process*, and *environment* by which an individual or group produces a *perceptible product* that is both novel and useful as define within a *social context*" (90). While some tests cut across the areas, most tests are specific to one of your familiar friends, the Four Ps.

Assessments of the **creative person** are often personality tests in which individuals are self-rated or rated by others as possessing/not possessing an inventory of traits associated with creative people. Teresa Amabile proposes that three variables are necessary for creativity: domain-relevant skills (what is important in one area might not be in another), creativity relevant skills (skills that cut across most domains), and intrinsic motivation (enjoyment of the task vs. demands from outside the person) (*Social; Creativity in Context*).

Assessments of the **creative process** are often divergent thinking tests in which the takers are asked to generate a quantity of responses to a problem (e.g., where are you going on vacation this year?) Perhaps the most famous of such instruments is the Torrance Tests for Creative Thinking (Torrance) that contains many scores, but the three most important are generally regarded as:

- **ideational fluency**: the number of generated ideas

- **originality**: the number of generated ideas not generated by students of the same age

- **flexibility**: the number of different idea categories.

Assessments of the **creative product** center on the things people make, tangibles such as a short story or a new smartphone. A popular method in this area is the Consensual Assessment Technique (CAT) wherein experts rate the amount of creativity on some sort of scale. You've probably seen this method loosely applied in TV shows such as *American Idol* or *Dancing with the Stars*. The problem here is that the "experts" do not have a pre-established rubric (if these rubrics exist, they have never been made available to the public, and "Yo, dog, you're in it to win it" has more entertainment than evaluative value) that sets up categories and values within those categories. On the other hand, you may have had papers in your gen ed courses evaluated according to expertly created rubrics that are not only available but used in class. Advanced classes in music, art, and creative writing tend to use these rubrics, which are usually made available at the beginning of the semester.

Assessments of the **creative press**, the last of the Big C assessments, focus on the environment, which may be the home, the classroom, or the workplace. Studies of the home could center on the roles of the parents, the child's relationship in the birth order (e.g., first, last), or even childhood traumas (e.g., death of a parent). Mihaly Csikszentmihalyi developed the Systems Model that sees creativity resulting from the interaction of a specific domain (e.g., English), the field (e.g., critics and editors), and the person. Perhaps the best known instrument for judging the workplace, KEYS: Assessing the Campus for Creativity, was developed by Theresa Amabile and others to rate an organization's environmental factors, such as encouraging risk-taking, rewarding creativity, providing resources, and offering healthy competition ("Assessing").

"Little c" assessment is the less formal type you perform on a daily basis without the help of a pre-established rubric. In fact, you cannot be truly creative without making some judgments along the way, or as Sir Ken Robinson states, "Being creative involves several processes that interweave within each other. The first is generative. The second is evaluative" (152).

To understand why judgment or critical thinking is necessary to the individual ideator, let's return to the nub of our definition of creative thinking. Do you remember the two essential traits, being novel and useful? Eventually the ideator has to make a call on whether the created process or product has these two essential traits. To be novel it must be original, and to be useful it has to go beyond novelty. Thus, some scheme of critical thinking must be employed, which is why critical thinking need not be creative, but all creative thinking is at some point critical thinking (though we admit that sometimes the critical thinking is supplied by an outside entity beyond the self, such as a teacher, a recording company, or even the patent office).

Some critical thinking schemes already exist, so one may or may not be applicable. One of the most pervasive critical thinking apparatuses found on college campuses is that provided by the Foundation for Critical Thinking with their eight Parts of Thinking (Elements of Thought), their nine Intellectual Standards, and their eight Intellectual Traits (Elder and Paul). However, such a vast scheme can often be cumbersome and unnecessary. Likewise, knowledge of the basic logical fallacies is helpful, but you probably won't be attempting to apply all of them as you proceed through your project. More often, you will be asking yourself simpler questions as you develop a germ of an idea, such as: Does it work? Is it useful? Is it logical? Does it hold together?

Assessment is used not only at the end of the creative thinking process, but also along the way at countless points. One of the first judgments made is often on the nature of the creative environment. Charlie and Hal found their university office so non-conducive to writing that they motored over to the local McDonald's for twenty years, and as work-at-home becomes more commonplace, the creation of a home-office space takes on more importance.

A second pre-process assessment is motivation. While much motivation is extrinsic, and raises and high grades incentivize, research shows that if even a part of your reason for undertaking a project is intrinsic, you will do better.

And how about exercising your judgment on your project goal. The more clearly you can define your purpose, hypothesis, or thesis, the better your chances. Now you are into the creative process where you will have to make lots of mini-assessments.

Some of the time you will have a formal project, but creativity is often needed in less formal, everyday "projects." In the next chapter, "Putting It All Together," we'll discuss a formal project where assessment is a continuing task throughout the entire effort, but what about less formal applications of creative thinking?

For instance, it's the weekend and you and a bunch of friends have gotten together to play a little softball. You don't have a regulation field because cars are parked in right, no umpires have been scheduled, and all eighteen players needed for a regulation game haven't shown. The only way to play is to make up some rules beyond the old sandlot favorite, the do-over. You outlaw hits to right (foul balls). You forbid stealing because you don't have a catcher (or necessary equipment for that matter) ... obviously no bunting. Everybody gets a maximum of ten pitches as balls and strikes aren't called. So you start with these "rules" and you adjust as the game goes on. What happens, for instance, when the ball goes down a rabbit hole? Ground-rule double?

If throughout the softball game you constantly create new rules to keep the game going, you'll find it easier if you determine what are the assessing principles at the core of your "project." Number one on your unofficial rubric is probably fairness—neither team should gain an undue advantage. Closely related to number one is amicability—the game is a friendly contest where the main object is to have fun, not to advance to the World Series of Softball. A third rule might be safety. If you pitch from the regulation forty-five feet and are throwing fast pitch, someone could get hurt, so you choose slo-pitch. And, of course, in the end flexibility is important; if a rule doesn't work, you change it or fall back on the all-important do-over rule.

Play ball!

Creative Concepts

- **"Big C" assessment** is formal, has a test specifically designed for an objective, and is performed by experts attempting to measure the Four Ps.

- **"Little c" assessment** is informal, has no specified test, and is undertaken by would-be creators in order to render a judgment on their ideas, their processes, their products, and/or their environments.

- **A rubric** of assessment guidelines is necessary in both types of assessment.

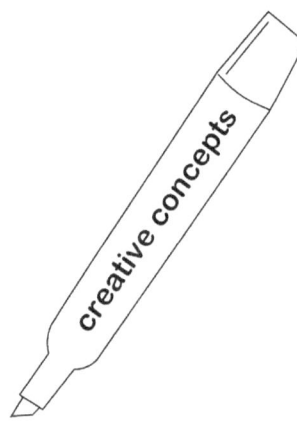

Exercises

1. Do a personal inventory. What kind of assessments do you use in your daily life? Do you decide things on a whim or do you have an established set of "rules" you follow? How do you resolve conflicts between the reasonable thing to do and what you want to do? Between demands of the job (whether school or employment) and the pull of family and friends? Between what you can afford and the lure of credit? Being aware of your "rules" will help you when it comes time to make decisions in creative and critical projects. Knowing your tendencies will help you with self-characterization (for instance, do you see yourself as a risk-taker?).

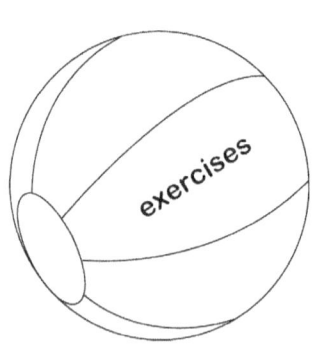

2. Do a personal inventory about an action you've taken in the last week. In retrospect, was your action effective? If given the chance for a "do-over," would you change anything? Why? Why not?

References

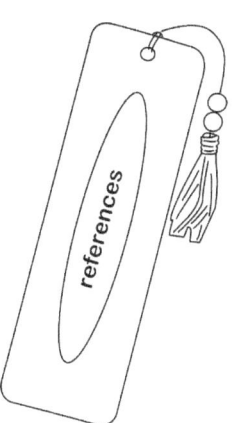

Amabile, Teresa. *The Social Psychology of Creativity*. New York: Springer Verlag, 1986. Print.

---. *Creativity in Context: Update to "The Social Psychology of Creativity."* Boulder: Westview Press, 1996. Print.

Amabile, Teresa, Regina Conti, Heather Coon, Jeffrey Lazenby, and Michael Herron. "Assessing the Work Environment for Creativity." *Academy of Management Journal* 39.5 (1996): 1154-84. *JSTOR*. Web. 11 Oct. 2011.

Csikszentmihalyi, Mihaly. *Creativity*. New York: HarperCollins, 1996. Print.

Elder, Linda, and Richard Paul. *The Aspiring Thinker's Guide to Critical Thinking*. Dillon Beach, CA: Foundation for Critical Thinking, 2009. Print.

Plucker, Jonathan, Ronald Beghetto, and Gayle Dow. "Why Isn't Creativity More Important to Educational Psychologists? Potential, Pitfalls, and Future Directions in Creativity Research." *Educational Psychologist* 39 (2004): 83-96. Print.

Robinson, Ken. *Out of Our Minds*. Hoboken: John Wiley & Sons, 2011. Print.

Torrance, E. *The Torrance Tests of Creative Thinking: Norms-Technical Manual*. Bensenville, IL: Scholastic Testing Service, 2008. Print.

Synthesizing: Putting It All Together

Cue "Mission Impossible" theme.

"Good morning. Your mission, should you choose to accept it, is to enter the International Magnificent Paper Airplane Contest (IMPAC). You will assemble your Impossible Missions Force (IMF) to design, build, and fly your model. Your goal will be to win one of two categories: Longest Flight in Distance or Longest Time in Flight. Should you or any member of your IM Force fail, your instructor will disavow any knowledge of your actions. Good luck."

All assignments have a starting point. Where's yours? Assembling your team? Finding the best environment to work in? Getting a clarification of the assignment's two possible goals? Finding the best possible paper to use? Heading directly to Wikipedia? Writing off your free time for the rest of the semester?

As the previous chapters have stressed, creative thinking is a **process**, but what we haven't done is suggest what that process may look like when you begin to utilize and combine the basic strategies. One of those previous chapters, however, focused on recognizing patterns, so perhaps as you have been reading, working with, and communicating about creative thinking, you have begun the difficult task of synthesizing the material into some helpful process of your own. In an interview with Amy Azzam, creativity expert Sir Ken Robinson underscores the need for a process: "A creative process may begin with a flash of a new idea or with a hunch. It may just start as noodling around with a problem, getting some fresh ideas along the way. It's a process, not a single event, and genuine creative processes involve critical thinking as well as imaginative insight and fresh ideas" (Azzam 23).

And why is the process important? The more you do it, the better at it you will become, as you probably have figured via the theory of **deliberate practice** (which we mentioned earlier). As David Kelley, founder of the design firm IDEO puts it, "Innovators aren't exceptional as much as they are confident" (Geer R5). Developing Creative Thinking Literacy, the knowledge and the practice with the skills, makes you more confident, which in a chicken-egg situation makes you better with the skills.

So what does that creative process look like? Historically some researchers have argued that creative cognition does not differ substantially from standard cognition (Gardner) and that it's the special combinations and patterns of the former that define creative thought. To generalize, the creative thinking process involves various stages that might be sequential or recursive. One of the earliest cognitive theorists, Wallas, suggested a four-stage process:

1. Preparation: definition of the problem and research

2. Incubation: not directly thinking about solutions

3. Illumination: an insight

4. Verification: testing the solution.

As you can see, this early 20th-Century theory appears very linear and doesn't take into account recursivity. By the end of the century, Teresa Amabile (Hennessey and Amabile) offered a componential model with three facets:

- Domain-relevant skills (e.g., knowledge of the domain)

- Creativity-relevant skills (e.g., see previous chapters)

- Task motivation.

Creative Problem Solving (CPS), started by brainstorming ad executive Alex Osborn, has a long history and many variations. Liang Zeng, Robert Proctor, and Gavriel Salvendy believe that "The creative process can be conceived of as a form of problem-defining and problem solving that follows the general model of problem analysis, ideation, evaluation, and implementation" (26). Other approaches analyze the methods used by artists (remember the "P" that stood for **person**?) from film to poetry to sculpture. While some theorists find specific approaches common to persons and others to domains, some emphasize the role of environment (remember the "P" for **press**?).

More fluid processes are often advanced. Thomas Ward and Yuliya Kolomyts point to the Geneplore model:

> [the Geneplore model] characterizes the development of novel and useful ideas as resulting from the interplay of *generative* processes that produce candidate ideas of varying degrees of creative potential and *exploratory* processes that expand on the potential. Rather than focusing on *the* creative process as a singular entity, the model identifies a cluster of basic cognitive processes, which combine in a variety of ways to influence the probability of a creative outcome. (94)

In discussing functional creativity (vs. aesthetic creativity), which is focused on creating concrete and useful products, David Cropley and Arthur Cropley "regard a seven-phase model as most appropriate" (310):

- Preparation: knowledge

- Activation: awareness of problems

- Generation: production of solutions

- Illumination: identifying key solution(s)

- Verification: promising solution proved useful

- Communication: mature solution presented to others

- Validation: expert feedback. (312)

In simplifying the research, we may be more confusing than illuminating. In truth researchers have come at it from many domains this past century in trying to understand creative thinking systems. As you get into these fields, you will learn their approaches. What we propose is a domain-general system for putting together what we have discussed in previous chapters into a system/model/process that will help you accomplish your difficult mission of constructing a paper airplane that will effectively meet your goals, but we're going to leave you alone on two of your choices, environment or collaborators, as often in academia and even business these choices are made by your instructor/assignment. For instance, the charge at the beginning of this chapter tells you to collaborate, but it does not explain how you select members or how many you select.

We suggest a five-phase approach:

- **Preparation**

- **Generation**

- **Tentative Selection**

- **Verification**

- **Refinement**

Phase I: Preparation

1. **Define your goals clearly**. Notice your mission provided you with two goals. Are duration and distance actually the same objective? If they are different, do you want to design one plane that could win both, or would you rather concentrate on winning just one of the two goals? Is your goal to win

or just make a reasonable showing (wasn't it Fernando/Billy Crystal of *Saturday Night Live* fame who said, "It is better to look good than to feel good"?)?

2. **Acquire basic knowledge in the domain**. In order to define your goal, you may need more information about the rules of the IMPAC contest (e.g., Are other products like balsa, tape, paper clips, and glue permitted? If so, any limits? Is CAD software legal in the design process?). Next you will need some background information on what wags call *aerogami* (e.g., what is the Reynolds number, camber, lift, drag?). While you or your team will probably never become aeronautical engineers, a little knowledge is helpful.

Phase II: Generation

1. **Piggyback on previous designs**. Generate multiple designs. You could tweak an extant design with a slightly larger tail. Or maybe you could base your design on something very recent, such as a stealth fighter plane, the Nighthawk or Raptor.

2. Try to **recognize patterns** in award-winning aircraft. For instance, is there a minimum/maximum size to the wings/fuselage? Is there an optimum ratio between the wing and fuselage? Without much knowledge of aerodynamics and a minimum remembrance of math, you should be able to calculate areas and ratios.

3. Conversely, instead of going with success, you might want to play the rebel and **shift perception**. For instance, in building paper airplanes, you might have always folded the traditional 8½ x 11 sheet of paper the long way; you could try folding the short way, you might even try a different size of paper, or you might even want to combine two sheets of paper (if IMPAC rules so allow). Most paper aircraft employ flat parts, but you might try curving the paper for the wing, the fuselage, the tail, or all parts.

4. **Play**. When you made paper airplanes as a kid, you probably just did it without consulting anyone's expertise or learning a single principle of aerodynamics. Explore with some designs. Take risks. If one noses into the ground and another one spins out of control, then you've just learned two designs that won't work. **Play** is especially effective when you have no time constraints and teammates with whom to play.

5. **Brainstorm** the design. Think of all the possible designs with which you are familiar, and have your team-mates do the same. Then start pooling your information. Maybe someone in the team has a friend or sibling who's entered the IMPAC challenge before.

6. Try a **metaphor**. As in *Jeopardy*, choose the category "Things That Fly." Maybe last night you saw a bat or read a comic book where the Dark Knight Detective threw his "Batarang."

7. Hopefully, while you are employing one of these strategies, you find yourself in the **flow**. Here, as in brainstorming, you need to jot down your ideas. All your ideas. Don't kill them off too soon. Vegetable growers often plant two to three times the number of carrot seeds appropriate for the space. They let the seeds all mature, grow for a while, and later thin them out so only the largest survive. Destroying an idea too soon can have a negative effect on collaborators, not to mention flow, while letting all ideas live at first actually encourages greater production.

8. Often in the flow or in brainstorming, you **catch a glimmer** of an idea. Last week five of us were sitting around a table and brainstorming an idea for a website. However, only four of us were talking—one person in the group volunteered to take thorough notes on everything said. After we were finished and she began to read over what had been said, we noticed a couple of good, but thoroughly underdeveloped ideas. Catching glimmers is both recognizing the germ of an idea, but also honing in on it for further development.

Phase III: Tentative Selection

1. **Narrow down your possibilities**. Up to this point you have allowed all ideas to live, and through the processes of piggybacking, patterning, perception shifting, playing, brainstorming, flowing, and glimmer-catching, you have even generated additional options. Now to decide upon your ultimate flying machine, you must first try to limit these choices through a number of methods:

- With **voting** you hold an election, but since small teams could make the selected group too small, give each member 5-10 votes. When the ballot is over, rank the selections. The advantage of this method is that everyone's selection is given equal weight.

- With **advocacy** you have each team member champion one, two, or three selections and try to produce a convincing argument for acceptance. You might allow each member only one choice if you wish to speed up the process.

- With **hunching** you ask members which choice just "feels" right. A problem with the first two methods is they depend upon the strength of the majority or perhaps loudness/good debate skills, and we know we make many choices in life that we can't clearly articulate (maybe just catch a glimmer of). Artists can't always tell you why they chose a particular color or point of view, for instance, but when we regard a finished picture of Cezanne or a novel by Hemingway, we know they have a unified vision of life.

2. **Try "making" (as Sir Ken Robinson suggests) or generating a low-res prototype**. Before Henry James would write a complete novel, he often composed his "scenarios," which could be 20,000-word versions of perhaps what would become a 100,000-word story. Novelist Arthur Hailey (e.g., *Airport*, *Hotel*) taped note cards representing major scenes on the wall and to show his plot development, he connected his cards with different colored string. Picasso was famous for his sketches on napkins and matchbox lids. For years, architects started by making a rough sketch of a project, not worrying at first about the little details, but trying mainly to capture the major design features. From there, they built balsa and cardboard versions before they started to work on the real-scale buildings; then computer-assisted design (CAD) software allowed a paper version, and now architects can transmit their CAD drawings to printers with polymer reservoirs that allow the printers to create three-dimensional plastic versions of the design, complete with colors. With our IMPAC contest, creating three paper airplanes from the choices is not difficult.

Phase IV. Verification

1. **Make the best choice**. Using your standards, opt for the optimum option. How do you know what that is? While the standards you employ help, often your choice is your "best guess." On the other hand, if things don't work out, you can always make another choice.

2. **Assess**. Obviously you will need a rubric, even if it consists of a single standard, utility. In this case, you want to know: does our chosen paper airplane perform well? Or you might want to expand your rubric. Each year, for instance, The *Wall Street Journal* Technology Innovation Awards go to various categories, such as Computing Systems and Storage, Consumer Electronics, and Energy, but to assess the entries the judges used a three-criteria rubric:

1. "Does the innovation break with conventional ideas or processes in the field?"

2. "Does it go beyond marginal improvements on something that already exists?"

3. "Will it have a wide impact in its field or on future technology?" (Ledger R1)

In your judging you are interested in duration and distance, so these may be the two subcategories of your one standard, utility.

Phase V. Refinement

1. **Tweak your design**. Most likely, your assessment in Phase IV revealed a problem, slight or major, that you need to work on.

2. **Reassess your design**. While "Will it fly?" is often employed as a metaphor, here you actually need to test your product.

Will following this process guarantee you a win in the IMPAC contest? Of course not, but following the process will probably increase your odds. More importantly, the more often you practice the process, the better your chances of creating anything become.

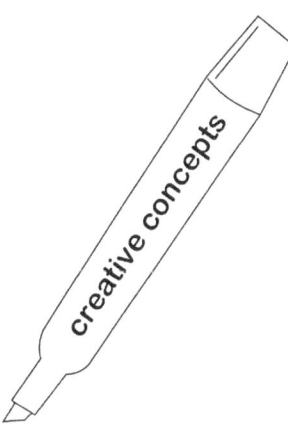

Creative Concepts

- Creative thinkers follow a process that is usually more recursive than linear.

- Creative processes vary in their phases, but utilize certain learnable skills.

- A good five-phase creative process for you to utilize consists of **Preparation**, **Generation**, **Tentative Selection**, **Verification**, and **Refinement**.

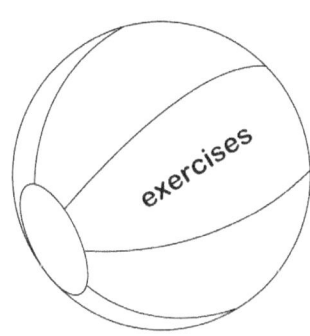

Exercises

1. Watch the movie *Apollo 13*. Note the process that Houston goes through when they realize ("Houston, we have a problem") the need to rescue the damaged space capsule. Can you spot the various phases of the engineers' cognitive processes?

2. Choose an "everyday" problem you've encountered in the last week. Use the five-phase creative process to arrive at a solution for the problem.

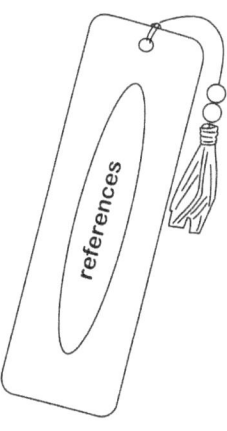

References

Azzam, Amy. "Why Creativity Now? A Conversation with Sir Ken Robinson." *Educational Leadership* 67.1 (2009): 22-26. Print.

Cropley, David, and Arthur Cropley. "Functional Creativity." *The Cambridge Handbook of Creativity*. Eds. James Kaufman and Robert Sternberg. Cambridge: Cambridge University Press, 2010. 301-317. Print.

Gardner, Howard. "Creativity: An Interdisciplinary Perspective." *Creativity Research Journal* 1.1 (1988): 8-26. Print.

Geer, Carolyn. "Innovation 101." *Wall Street Journal* 17 Oct. 2011: R5. Print.

Hennessey, Beth, and Teresa Amabile. "Consensual Assessment." *Encyclopedia of Creativity* I. Eds. Mark Runco and S. Pritzer. San Diego: Academic Press, 1999. 349-60. Print.

Leger, John. "The Wall Street Journal 2011 Technology Innovation Awards." *Wall Street Journal* 17 October 2011: R1. Print.

Osborn, Alex. *Applied Imagination*. New York: Scribner's, 1953. Print.

Wallas, Graham. *The Art of Thought*. New York: Harcourt Brace and World, 1926. Print.

Ward, Thomas, and Yuliya Kolomyts. "Cognition and Creativity." *The Cambridge Handbook of Creativity*. Ed. James Kaufman and Robert Sternberg. Cambridge: Cambridge University Press, 2010. 93-112. Print.

Zeng, Liang, Robert Proctor, and Gavriel Salvendy. "Can Traditional Divergent Thinking Tests Be Trusted in Measuring and Predicting Real-World Creativity?" *Creativity Research Journal* 23.1 (2011): 24-37. *EBSCOhost*. Web. 10 Oct. 2011.

Academizing Creative Thinking: The Creative Campus Movement

Throughout this book, we've provided a definition and context for creative thinking. Specifically, we've given you strategies for applying creative thinking in the classroom and beyond. You now know that creative thinking influences all aspects of academics and can help you develop leadership skills sought by the business world.

One of our goals for this collection, however, is to make creative thinking academic – that is, to integrate creativity into the curriculum. By academizing creative thinking, we also hope that it becomes centralized in your academic and professional career. We contend that creative thinking should serve as a lens through which you approach the decision-making and problem-solving processes. We also argue that creative thinking can enhance academic performance in the classroom as evidenced through the addition of programs geared toward fostering creative thinking. Furthermore, we see a number of benefits for making creative thinking intentional on our campuses:

- improved academic performance among students

- improved retention

- students who employ multiple lines of thinking for solving problems

- increased leadership potential.

And by campus, the creative campus movement means the entire campus, not just in its traditional venue of the arts. As Steven Tepper says, "Creativity thrives on those campuses where there is an abundant cross-cultural exchange and a great deal of 'border' activity between disciplines, where collaborative work is commonplace, risk taking is rewarded, failure is expected, and the creative arts are pervasive and integrated into campus life" (4). Elizabeth Long-Lingo and Steven Tepper elaborate: "While readers often jump to the conclusion that 'creative' applies only to the arts, leading programs focus on the creative process that threads through not only art and design, but also engineering, medicine, and the arts and sciences" (A28).

So, what's all this talk about academizing creative thinking about anyway? Well, we're glad you asked!

Academics have discussed creative thinking for many years. We've waged debates about what it is, exactly, how it should be taught, and how it impacts classroom spaces. There's little doubt that this subject has generated much discussion. These discussions are useless, however, without action. Creative thinking entails an action. It's the essence of creative thinking.

Let's unpack this point a bit more. Action implies making something. We know that creative products must be novel and useful, remember? We also know that creative products are the result of a great deal of thought. However, this kind of thinking might be different than from what you're accustomed to seeing in class or on campus. This kind of thinking is active; it shows engagement with a process and a product. It involves thinking with your hands.

So, what might thinking with your hands look like? You walk into the classroom. This classroom doesn't look like what you're accustomed to, though. There aren't any desks or rows. There are chairs with tablet arms. The professor has set up large sticky notes on the walls, and you have a few dry-erase boards. The class starts with a brief description of the day and a task: to make a product to be marketed to hospitals that will simplify operations of the room, a new remote control. You start by sketching out rough ideas with your small group. You go through four iterations – drawing the schematics quickly and generating ideas quickly. They take a rough, visual form – filling the walls with ideas for action. You then transition from your diagrams – with notes in hand – to the next phase.

Phase two involves generating prototypes. You now take your notes and stick them in on the wall in sequence. You combine a few elements of each for your prototype, a handle here, a button there, size, and color. You're ready to create – or **ACT**. The professor provides each group with a bin of tinker toys, LEGOs, rolls of tape, markers, crayons, and toothpicks, also known as the stuff of play. After talking through your schematic once more, you and your team begin to create a prototype. It doesn't look like much at first; really, just a jumbled mess. But you revise two or three times by undoing and redoing your artifact. It's an intellectual and physical act.

Creative thinking engages both idea development and generation along with the act of creating. You generate artifacts that will probably look much different than your traditional research paper, and the parameters will probably be much broader. While we are seeing many projects like this at EKU, in the Noel Studio, and on creative campuses throughout the country, we have not seen as much written about how to make creative thinking academic.

We argue that creative thinking can be academized by making it **intentional**. That is, we want to foster intentional creative thinking skills in students so you know when you're employing creative thinking skills and have more control over the available options for using creative thinking to develop products, skills, and practices. Once you have control over these skills, they'll become ingrained in all that you do – from collaborating with peers to making business decisions.

We argue that creative thinking should be taught, like writing or speaking, and that there's value in teaching these skills early on so that students can employ them throughout their college careers. So, what exactly should students be able to do if we're academizing creative thinking? We argue that students should:

- employ strategies of creative thinking

- choose the most effective strategy for the problem

- use creative thinking to engage productive group dynamics

- develop leadership skills based on creative thinking strategies

- realize opportunities to employ creative thinking

- teach creative thinking to others in a variety of business and academic settings.

One example of how creative thinking can be academized has taken place at Eastern Kentucky University – where we work. The Noel Studio for Academic Creativity fosters creative thinking by encouraging students to pursue multiple paths for their projects. That is, in the Noel Studio, students gain perspective on their communication pieces by considering all available options and audience members. Students might begin their experience by brainstorming ideas – or creating a mind map – and then drafting ideas in the Greenhouse. From there, students might design texts electronically using touch-screen monitors. Remember when we were talking about "thinking with your hands?" Well, here's a new take on that same concept. We've added technology that allows students to move electronic objects around on the monitor – creating an environment that engages students on many levels, in many ways.

To engage creative thinking, students must be able to think with their hands and minds – to **immerse** themselves within the process. Where we have fallen short in the past, though, is teaching students to articulate what creative thinking is and how to do it. Or how to articulate their creative approach. If you don't know what it is, or can't tell us what you're doing, creative thinking isn't *intentional*. It's just luck. We want creative thinking to become habit, but it cannot become part of your daily thinking unless you know what it is and how to channel it.

Let's explore methods for channeling that creativity, then:

- embrace divergent thinking when generating ideas

- approach brainstorming sessions and meetings with goals but give participants the freedom to share ideas willingly

- create an environment of inclusion and don't discount ideas until you've explored them fully

- communicate ideas by talking through them, noting them visually, and encouraging participants to take the lead

- encourage participation from team members.

William Klemm, a former Colonel in the U.S. Air Force, argues that, "Leaders should stimulate creativity for two very important reasons: to prevent obsolescence and to increase productivity" (449). Of course, we would agree completely. Creativity is important in all aspects of leadership—from decision-making to inspiring a team. As Klemm suggests, leaders must nurture creativity, which means creating an environment where team members are secure in sharing ideas and where there is time to meditate on ideas.

It all sounds simple, doesn't it? But it's really not. When you're attached to ideas and a successful outcome, it can be difficult to distance yourself, at times. That is, it can be challenging to give all ideas an honest chance to thrive. We argue that you need **divergent thinking**—which is generative in nature—before convergent thinking—which is evaluative. You need to generate ideas—and encourage many ideas brought forward by team members—before you can adequately evaluate them. All too often, however, we look for meaning before seeing the array of possibilities. We can't see true meaning without exploring connections, though, and we have to give those connections time to develop.

This chapter isn't simply a call for action. It's a call for intentional action that privileges creative thinking by providing space, time, and methods for it to occur through intentional moves—intellectual and physical. We argue, then, that creative thinking must be intentional in the classroom and that—when creativity is respected, if not encouraged—there are many opportunities for students to enhance their academic experience. Our call, then, is one that is political and cultural in nature. By academizing creative thinking, we hope that it becomes a day-to-day activity in the classroom and that our classroom environments—fostered by students and teachers side-by-side—become catalysts for creative activity.

We know that industry demands creative thinkers, and the ideal time to begin your journey is in the college classroom. These spaces of higher education, however, must encourage creative thinking to occur. Without spaces for cultivating creative thinking, we risk losing this opportunity to make it intentional.

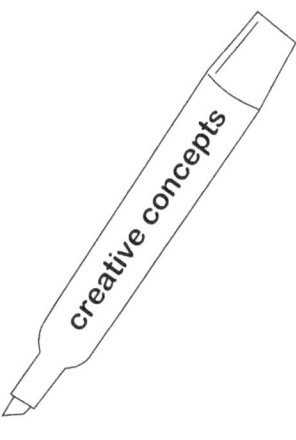

Creative Concepts

- A **Creative Campus** is one where creativity threads through all the disciplines, not just the arts, and collaboration between these disciplines is encouraged.

- Creative Thinking can help you develop leadership skills.

- Creative Thinking can enhance academic performance.

- Creative Thinking involves action.

- Creative Thinking should be intentional.

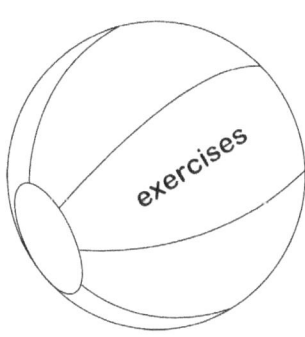

Exercises

1. Choose a project/paper/presentation you've completed for one of your classes. How could you have approached the assignment differently? How might this different approach have changed the final product?

2. Think about a test you've taken recently in one of your classes. Did the test reveal what you knew about the material? How could you have structured the test if you were the instructor? Why?

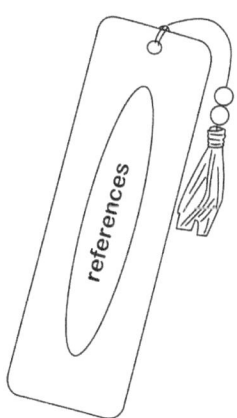

References

Klemm, William R. "Leadership: Creativity and Innovation." *Concepts of Air Force Leadership* Sept. 2001. Web. 10 Oct. 2011

Long-Lingo, Elizabeth, and Steven Tepper. "The Creative Campus: Time for a `C' Change." *The Chronicle of Higher Education* 15 Oct. 2010: A28-A29. Print.

Tepper, Steven. "Taking the Measure of the Creative Campus." *Peer Review* 8.2 (2006): 4-7. *EBSCOhost*. Web. 17 Oct. 2011.

Domain-Specific Creative Thinking

So far we have attempted to prepare you for a 21st Century that will, according to Erica McWilliam, Daniel Pink, Keith Sawyer, and others, demand a deeper understanding and more thorough nurturing of that creative impulse that dwells in each of us. To accomplish this rather formidable task, we have treated those most fundamental concepts and strategies you will need regardless of the career path you choose.

Steven Tepper and George Kuh summarize what they call "abilities and skills" that transcend disciplines, cultivating creativity regardless of one's field:

1. the ability to approach problems in nonroutine ways using analogy and metaphor;

2. conditional or abductive reasoning (posing "what if" propositions and reframing problems);

3. keen observation and the ability to see new and unexpected patterns;

4. the ability to risk failure by taking initiative in the face of ambiguity and uncertainty;

5. the ability to heed critical feedback to revise and improve an idea;

6. a capacity to bring people, power, and resources together to implement novel ideas; and

7. the expressive agility required to draw on multiple means (visual, oral, written, media-related) to communicate novel ideas to others." (B13)

Importantly, Tepper and Kuh suggest that an individual gains most from these abilities and skills by "deliberately practicing" them "over an extended period of time" (B13), a concept we have previously discussed. Their claim is consistent with studies finding that optimum creativity in any field requires a person to become an expert, investing around 10,000 hours (Ericsson) of deliberative study and practice.

Reaching your full creative potential, then, requires that you complement the basic abilities and skills encountered in this text with those more discipline-specific abilities and skills you will gain in your field of study. As Keith Sawyer sums up, "Creativity researchers have concluded that real-world creative performance depends both on domain-general creative skills, as well as domain-specific knowledge and skills. Although we don't yet know the exact balance, and although that balance probably varies across domains, the implications of this research are that creativity involves both general creativity skills and also domain specific skills" (6).

As you progress through the curriculum, moving from General Education courses through upper-division courses in your major, you will discover that your ability to think creatively depends on ever-more-specific knowledge and skill sets. James Kaufman, Jason Cole, and John Baer provide an informative insight into this progression with their Amusement Park Theoretical (APT) Model of Creativity:

> The APT Model is based on the metaphor [of] a large amusement park. In an amusement park there are initial requirements (e.g., ticket) that apply to all areas of the park. Similarly, there are initial requirements that, to varying degrees, are necessary to creative performance in all domains (e.g., intelligence, motivation). Amusement parks also have *general thematic areas* (e.g., at Disney World one might select among EPCOT, the Magic Kingdom, the Animal Kingdom, and Disney-MGM Studios), just as there are several different general areas in which someone could be creative (e.g., the arts, science). Once in one type of park, there are sections (e.g., Fantasyland, Tomorrowland), just as there are *domains* of creativity within larger *general thematic* areas (e.g., physics and biology are domains in the *general thematic* area of science). These domains in turn can be subdivided into *micro-domains* (e.g., in Fantasyland one might visit Cinderella's Castle or It's a Small World; in the domain of psychology, one might specialize in cognitive psychology or social psychology). (120)

Think of *Introduction to Applied Creative Thinking* as your ticket to the world of creative thinking!

Once inside this world, what can you expect as your courses become more specialized? Certainly, you will be able to continue using those fundamental strategies we've discussed earlier in the book, but what new skills might you encounter in your major field of study?

Obviously, we can't cover every potential major in the remainder of this chapter, but, perhaps, we can suggest some of the domain/content-specific strategies drawn from several disciplines.

Literature

While normally associated with *critical thinking*, the study of literature affords many opportunities for creative thought. Not only can an instructor employ creative strategies to enhance teaching effectiveness, but a truly creative instructor can foster student creativity by providing opportunities for them to engage material in new, sometimes unexpected ways. More than simply fun, these approaches can draw out those creative impulses that make students co-facilitators of learning in the class.

Take, for example, a lit class on Henrik Ibsen's famous 19th-Century play *Hedda Gabler*. Anyone from experienced scholar to novice student who studies the drama must ultimately confront the work's pivotal question: why would a woman who seemingly has everything for which an aristocrat of her day could wish put a pistol to her head and pull the trigger?

Sure, the instructor might take the traditional approach to the material and present a lecture on 19th-Century Norwegian morés followed by a quick Q&A on the play's characters and plot and a wrap-up in which the instructor presents a research-supported answer.

But what if in the spirit of television's CSI and all its crime scene investigation counterparts the instructor chose to involve the students in determining the cause of suicide by convening a coroner's inquest during which the students could ask a parade of the play's characters questions concerning their knowledge of Hedda's final act? This approach would necessitate students' use of fundamental creative strategies, such as **glimmer**, **collaboration**, **piggybacking**, and **perception-shift** as well as knowledge and creative skills specific to the field. Critical thinking might help you develop a scholarly frame of mind, but you would also need a thorough knowledge of the conventions of literature (whether creative of not): character, plot setting, method of narration, and theme. In some subfields you would need to be versed on the poetics of poetry, the conventions of pop lit, and even theories of rhetoric and linguistics.

Science

The discipline has long been plagued by a traditional approach to learning that involves lecture and regimented laboratory experimentation, but as Christopher Longo asserts, "The days of lecturing are over. *Inquiry-based science* instruction is at the forefront of instructional practice" (55). "This approach," continues Largo, "allows learning to be hands on, rigorous, and application-based" (56). Further, this strategy calls on students "to take more responsibility for the problems they chose to solve" and even though they "will make mistakes and attempt to solve inconsequential or even wrongly posed problems...as they learn from their mistakes" (Sternberg & Lubar 170).

Lee Gass claims that not allowing freedom to err inhibits "development of creative problem-solving skills" (3). Gass illustrates this point by referring to two students who, after reading a research article on conduction of sound by bone and designing and performing their own experiments, concluded the article's main point was wrong. After several follow-up experiments, the students were confident that they had proven their point. Only after realizing that they had made an incorrect assumption about the article's point on bone conduction (they had assumed the article meant all bone conducts sound rather than solely skull bone) did they comprehend their error. According to Gass,

> The boys' conclusion was wrong. But there was something right about what they did to reach it. Most of their deductive logic was solid, and their experimental design, the care that they took in executing it, and how they interpreted their results were flawless... But for that critical assumption in a critical place, the boys were impeccable creative scientists... .

The inquiry-based approach is but one of the creativity-enhancing strategies being introduced into the 21st-Century science classroom. The *science content-based* approach calls on students to use creative writing involving analogies to foster imagination. Per Morten Kind and Vanessa Kind as well as Alane Starko hold that this type of imagination can give both better understanding and new perspectives on scientific subjects.

Vivien Cheng concludes, "creative writing is considered as an effective strategy for enhancing students' imagination, creative thinking and also understanding of science concepts."

The *science scenario* approach involves creative problem solving to foster creativity. Scott Isakksen, Brian Dorval, and Donald Treffanger describe treating open-ended problems that call for creative solutions as a six stage process involving mess-finding, data-finding, problem-finding, idea-finding, solution-finding, and acceptance-finding—each stage calling for both divergent and convergent thinking. And a colleague of ours in biology recently told us the scientific method of investigating has been replaced by critical thinking.

The 21st-Century science classroom is an arena where both traditional and new concepts meet with creativity-fostering teaching approaches to ready students for an ever-evolving world.

Music

Music, as an art, has always been considered a discipline where only the most creative dwell. Too many times, however, student creativity has been taken for granted. David Brinkman claims that in the field, "Teaching others to become more creative is a step that many teachers do not take" (49). To illustrate what he believes needs to be done toward a future where "creativity will be more of an expectation" (50), he describes a scenario wherein a music teacher has a band in which instrumentation isn't balanced because of too many percussionists and too few trumpets. Not being able to find music to fit the band's makeup, the instructor could come up with possible solutions on his/her own, thus demonstrating a creative approach to teaching. But what if she decides to teach her students <u>for</u> creativity?

Brinkman's answer encapsulates much of the new, problem-solving approach being used in the contemporary music classroom.

1. Outline the problem to the students…Do the students know their band is not balanced? Do they understand issues of seniority, blend, harmony, school performance expectations and literature?

2. Help students generate some ideas of what can be done to fix the problem.

3. Help students with their solutions. If the solution is to write some new music, then they will need some skills in motivation. Could they generate a new piece of music "by ear?" A well-structured adventure in writing music could be infinitely motivating. Could students produce a totally unexpected idea, such as interacting with another band via new Internet technologies?

4. Solve the problem using student-generated solutions. The students need to develop the expertise, motivation, and creative thinking skills necessary… .(50)

As with other disciplines, music demands new approaches involving both general and domain-specific creativity.

Mathematics

Much like the natural sciences, mathematics has not been traditionally associated with creativity, with the possible exception of those geniuses, such as Pythagoras, Newton, and Einstein, who have carved their names into the history books. But, as Dylan would say, "The times, they are a changin.'" Atara Shriki asserts, "It is widely agreed that mathematics students of all levels should be exposed to thinking creatively and flexibly about mathematical concepts and ideas" (159).

As opposed to the old-school approach that passed on opportunities to engage students with open-ended problems or allow them to fail after extended periods of independent work, the 21st-Century classroom, according to Eric Mann, should engage students in active problem solving and creative exploration that will allow them to understand the essence of the concepts involved. Further, Bharath Sriraman calls for intellectual risk-taking on the part of students and active sharing of insights gained. Mann even suggests that students be allowed to design and answer their own mathematical problems rather than be tied to tried-and-true workbook materials.

While some disagreement exists in the field over exactly what constitutes creativity, how creativity should be assessed, and if creativity in mathematics is mainly domain specific, general, or some combination of the two, little argument remains over the need to ask students to assume increased responsibility in the learning process—an act requiring the application of creative thinking.

Our review has barely scratched the surface of what's going on across the disciplines concerning creativity, but, perhaps, it suggests your need to embrace the principles of creative thinking, both domain general and domain specific, regardless of your intended major.

Creative Concepts

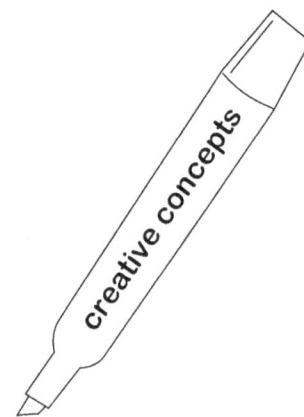

- Both general and domain-specific creativity are necessary regardless of one's intended major field of study.

- **Domain-specific creativity** demands thorough knowledge of the discipline's content.

- The more specialized your study becomes, the more domain-specific your creative thinking must become.

- **Deliberate practice** of 10,000 hours is necessary to increase your expertise in a domain.

Exercises

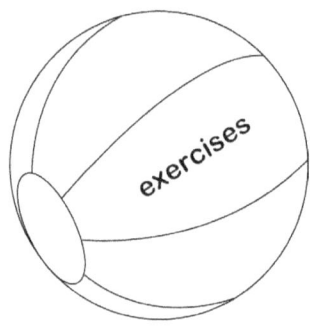

1. Create a scenario involving a real-life problem you might encounter at the University. How would you view the problem from the perspective of a general education student? How might your view change if you adopted the perspective of a math major? a sociology major? an English major? What about your solution to the problem?

2. Create a Venn Diagram showing the relationship of domain-general creative thinking skills you've learned in this class with those domain-specific skills you expect to encounter in your major.

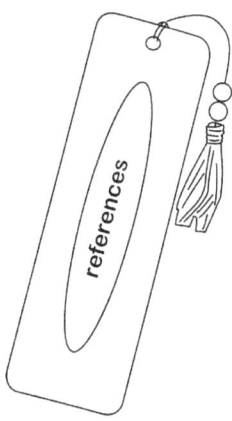

References

Brinkman, David. "Teaching Creativity and Teaching for Creativity." *Arts Education Policy Review* 111.2 (2010): 48-59. *EBSCOhost*. Web. 11 Oct. 2011.

Cheng, Vivian. "Teaching Creative Thinking in Regular Science Lessons: Potentials and Obstacles of Three Difference Approaches in an Asian Context." *Asia-Pacific Forum in Science, Learning and Teaching*, 11.1 (2010): Article 17, 1-21. Web. 12 Oct. 2011.

Ericsson, K. Anders. "Attaining Excellence Through Deliberate Practice: Insights from the Study of Expert Performance." *The Pursuit of Excellence in Education*. Ed. M. Ferrari. Hillsdale, NJ: Erlbaum, 2002. 21-55. Print.

Gass, Lee. "Teaching for Creativity in Science: An Example." *Creativity at Work* July 1998. Web. 12 Oct. 2011.

Isaken, Scott, Brian Dorval, and Donald Treffinger. *Creative Approaches to Problem Solving: A Framework for Innovation and Change*. Williamsville, NY: Creative Problem Solving Group-Buffalo, 2000. Print.

Kaufman, James, Jason Cole, and John Baer. "The Construct of Creativity: Structural Models for Self-Reported Creativity Ratings." *Journal of Creative Behavior* 43.2 (2009): 119-32. *GoogleScholar*. Web. 11 Oct. 2011.

Kind, Per Morten, and Vanessa Kind. "Creativity in Science Education: Perspectives and Challenges for Developing School Science." *Studies in Science Education* 43.1 (2007): 1-37. *GoogleScholar*. Web. 11 October 2011.

Longo, Christopher. "Fostering Creativity or Teaching to the Test? Implications of State Testing on the Delivery of Science Instruction." *Clearing House* 83.2 (2010): 54-57. *EBSCOhost*. Web. 11 Oct. 2011.

Mann, Eric. "Creativity: The Essence of Mathematics." *Journal for the Education and the Gifted*, 30.2 (2006): 236-60. Print.

McWilliam, Erica. *The Creative Workforce*. Sydney: UNSW, 2008. Print.

Pink, Daniel. *A Whole New Mind: Moving From the Information Age to the Conceptual Age*. New York: Penguin, 2005. Print.

Sawyer, Keith. "A Call to Action: The Challenge of Creative Teaching and Learning." To appear in *Teachers College Record*, 2011. Web. 14 Oct. 2011. <http://www.artsci.wustl.edu/~ksawycr/PDFs/TCR.pdf>.

Shriki, Atara. "Working Like Real Mathematicians: Developing Prospective Teachers' Awareness of Mathematical Creativity Through Generating New Concepts." *Education Studies in Mathematics* 73.2 (2010): 159-79. *EBSCOhost*. Web. 16 Oct. 2011.

Sriraman, Bharath. "The Characteristics of Mathematical Creativity." *2DM Mathematics Education* 41.1-2 (2009): 13-27. Print.

Starko, Alane Jordan. *Creativity in the Classroom: Schools of Curious Delight*. New York: Routledge, 2010. Print.

Sternberg, Robert, and Todd Lubart. "Creating Creative Minds." *Contemporary Issues in Curriculum*. Eds. A. Ornstein, E. Pajak, and S. Ornstein. Boston: Allyn & Bacon, 2007. 169-78. Print.

Tepper, Steven, and George Kuh. "Let's Get Serious About Creating Creativity." *The Chronicle Review* 9 Sept. 2011: B13-14. Print.

Creative Thinking and Digital Media

As a student, you are probably interested in, perhaps even fascinated with, learning more about digital media. Imagine, though, instead of attending a passive lecture, in a traditional lecture hall, you enter to a room with a cluster of monitors on the wall where you access an interactive site. It looks like just a blank space, as no keyboards are noticeable. Wait a minute, though. Your classmate touches the monitor. It lights up with a series of icons. Your turn. You quickly take to this new digital space, using it to sketch out that next project you were having a hard time getting into.

Actually, this space isn't just found in your imagination. In fact, it's rather common in environments such as the Noel Studio. Its Greenhouse has a monitor wall with touch-screen technologies where students create visual and even interactive messages with digital media.

Yes, technology can enhance creative thinking, in the classroom and in the workplace. Exploring the relationship between technology and his concept of remix, Lawrence Lessig suggests that remix – an alternative text made from an original – is part of the creative process. It resembles standing on the shoulders of giants (remember Isaac Newton's metaphor?) and **piggybacking** through the use of technology. The act, or art, necessarily involves composing with digital media: video and audio, communications of a digital nature that integrate the visual, oral, and aural. Lessig advocates for a culture of creativity (*Remix* 18), linking creativity – especially remix – to freedom. We agree. Intellectual freedom, which can also be rigorous, is directly linked to your creative thinking. The key, though, is to unlock that capacity. While we would not dare suggest that the mere use of technology itself enhances creative thinking, we do argue that creative thinking about technology can provide ample opportunity for students to shift perspective about their audience, purpose, context, and ultimately the persuasive appeal of a product.

Let's take, for example, Lessig's well-known TED Talk on the "laws that choke creativity." In it, Lessig provides several examples of remix, all of which involve creative uses of technology, such as a new video with a familiar song or a new song set behind a classic film. In both cases, the meaning changes. Want a closer look? Take a few minutes to check out Lessig's examples in "Re-examining Remix" (http://www.ted.com/talks/lessig_nyed.html). What do you notice?

1) They're videos?

2) They're video with familiar audio (music)?

Sure, that's a start, but keep going. In this video, Lessig explains that remix is the use of video technologies to provide a new slant. In fact, he suggests that technology allows us to say things differently. Video – and other digital media, according to Lessig – have become "tools of creativity" or "tools of speech," as he details in this video speech. He continues by explaining that this is how our generation speaks. In other words, as Lessig argues in *Remix*, "Like a great essay or a funny joke, a remix draws upon the work of others in order to do new work. It is great writing without words. It is creativity supported by a new technology" (108).

Many students are being asked to compose through digital media, especially with emerging spaces, such as the emerging Noel Studio for Academic Creativity at EKU. This change in media does not and has not meant relaxation of academic rigor. Not at all. Students are being asked to think creatively about their use of technology, to break free from traditional attitudes about the modes and media employed.

Creative thinking, through the use of technology, entails a good deal of flexibility. Moreover, creative thinking in digital media might be regarded as visual thinking. To draw from Cynthia Selfe, creative thinking as designed through digital media could include "visual poems, visual essays, visual messages, visual arguments, collages, multimedia presentations, among other forms" (69). In the Noel Studio, for instance, students have used a variety of digital media to design innovative and effective products that meet complex challenges. Example projects include oral communication scenarios for college students developed using a popular movie maker called Xtranormal or even using a video to announce an event, rather than traditional flyers, as Shawn Apostel did for the Noel Studio's communication awards (http://eku-class.blogspot.com/2011/08/introducing-noel-studio-public-speaking.html) or an online exhibit developed in Second Life (http://www.youtube.com/watch?v=ehSeGeBAbzQ). Technology has included:

- Installations in Second Life, a virtual immersive world (http://secondlife.com/)

- Videos in Xtranormal (http://www.xtranormal.com/)

- Moving presentations in Prezi (http://prezi.com/)

Of course, students now have access to a variety of free online spaces for storing videos, digital stories, and visual poems:

- YouTube (http://www.youtube.com/)

- Vimeo (http://vimeo.com/)

James Paul Gee, in *What Video Games Have to Teach Us About Learning and Literacy*, explores literacy skills through the lens of video games. Storytelling, as we know, engages creativity. It involves spontaneous thinking, imagery, metaphor, and **perception shift**. It also utilizes **piggybacking**, **catching glimmers**, and **play**, concepts we have explored in a variety of ways previously. Janet Murray, for example, coined the term "cyberdrama," as Noah Wardrip-Fruin and Pat Harrigan tell us in their introduction to *First Person* (1) to describe these new genres.

So, what does this new creative composition look like? It's complex, to be quite honest, and will require a great deal of trial and error. Do you recall when we discussed creative thinking as the act of creation – making something that is unique and yet has value? Well, let's start there. Janet Murray's cyberdramas, or digital stories, might involve a few component parts, right? Let's see if we can name a few:

- characters

- plot

- setting

And what else? Now let's consider your audience:

- What do you want to communicate?

- What do you want audience members to think or know?

Now let's look at the available digital media:

- What available technologies will allow you to create your message or story?

- Is there a format that will make your message more compelling or convincing?

- How will audience members access this digital product?

What if your instructor pointed you to a video about the syllabus for your next class, rather than lecturing you on the benefits of reading it, as Shawn Apostel does here with his public speaking class: http://ekuclass.blogspot.com/2011/08/some-helpful-links-for-class-this.html?

Your decisions will affect the ultimate success – convincingness, effectiveness, or marketability of your digital media product. As has been the case with students at EKU, designing creative products through digital media is not easy. In fact, many have said that designing a creative product that involves digital media is more challenging than writing a traditional research paper. It's not always comfortable, and you'll certainly go through several iterations of your product. Keep in mind these issues are all part of the creative process. Composing with digital media is not intended to solve all of your problems or to make your life easier. That's not the point at all. We know that readers consume media in multiple forms. With the proliferation of social media, a video is more easily distributed and serves a different purpose than a newspaper.

To employ creative thinking to its fullest extent when designing with digital media, you must take into consideration the situational factors involved, which would include your goals for designing the product in the first place and what issue it's supposed to resolve. Think back to Shawn's Xtranormal videos and how much more interesting it was to watch them than listen to a lecture.

What's the key to incorporating digital media successfully? It's your audience, purpose, and context for creating the product.

When working with digital media, it's important to approach the process with an adventurous spirit. You're going to revise. You're going to pursue multiple paths. But the beauty of composing with digital media is the multiple opportunities to explore before you identify the best solution. The process doesn't involve the use of technology just because it's available. Not at all. Your success will be determined by the process you follow through creative thinking.

Remember Lessig's "remix?" Composing with digital technologies might mean crafting two ideas into one, merging multiple paths, or combining video and audio in new ways. The important point to remember is your message. For example, take an old family video, analyze what it was about—time, event, people, and purpose for the video—and overlay music to it. I bet the message changes. It might change with each audio selection. But what does it say? What's your intention? A simple message can be more impactful than an overly and unnecessarily complex one. A short video can capture an audience's attention and convey your point with more power than a twenty-minute video. Advertisements, for example, are short and get right to the point. They make you think while attempting to convince you to think a certain way. Your digital products should be created with purpose, engaging a full invention and revision process.

Working with digital media can be enlightening and can provide you with creative experiences and opportunities that you've not had before. You'll have the chance to craft messages using images, videos, and music that can convey powerful messages not available in a single mode or media. We encourage you to experiment and plan ahead. Take the time to enjoy the creative process!

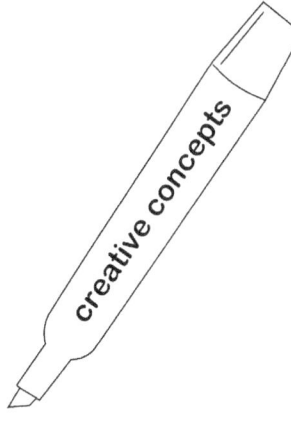

Creative Concepts

- Technology can enhance creative thinking.

- **Remix** – an alternative text constructed from an original source – is part of the creative process.

- Intellectual freedom is linked to creative thinking.

- A change in media presentation DOES NOT represent a relaxation of intellectual rigor.

- The key to incorporating digital media into a presentation involves audience, purpose, and context.

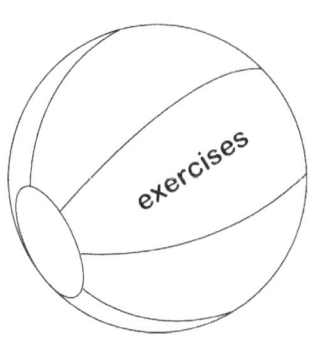

Exercises

1. Think about an essay you've written recently. How could you have presented it via digital media? Would the new mode of presentation have enhanced your presentation's effect? How?

2. Create a music video for your favorite rock song. What would the the scenery look like? How would the players be dressed? What actions would occur? Do any striking images come to mind?

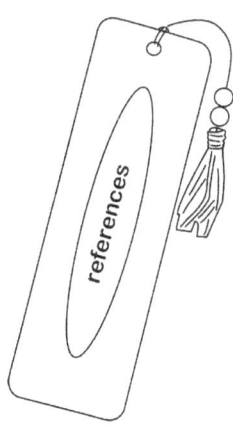

References

Apostel, Shawn. EKU Public Speaking Competition. 17 Aug. 2011. Web. 25 Oct. 2011. <http://www.xtranormal.com/watch/12381486/public-speaking-competition>.

---. EKU Public Speaking. Read the Syllabus. 22 Aug. 2011. Web. 25 Oct. 2011. <http://www.xtranormal.com/watch/12392831/read-the-syllabus>.

Gee, James Paul. *What Video Games Have to Teach Us About Learning and Literacy*. New York: Palgrave, 2003. Print.

Lessig, Lawrence. *Remix: Making Art and Commerce Thrive in the Hybrid Economy*. New York: Penguin, 2008. Print.

---. "Larry Lessig on Laws that Choke Creativity." *Ted Talk*. March 2007. Web. 15 October 2011<http://www.ted.com/talks/larry_lessig_says_the_law_is_strangling_creativity.html>.

---."Re-Examining Remix." *Ted Talk*. Apr. 2010. Web. 22 Oct. 2011. <http://www.ted.com/talks/lessig_nyed.html>.

Selfe, Cynthia. "Toward New Media Texts: Taking Up the Challenges of Visual Literacy." In *Writing New Media: Theory and Applications for Expanding Teachings of Composition*. Eds. Anne Francis Wysocki, Johndan Johnson-Eilola, Cynthia L. Selfe, and Geoffrey Sirc. Logan: USUP, 2004. Print.

Wardrip-Fruin, Noah, and Pat Harrington. "Cyberdrama." *First Person: New Media as Story, Performance, and Game.* Eds. Noah Wardrip, Pat Harrington, and Michael Crumpton. Cambridge: MIT P, 2004. Print.

The Creative Class: Creative Thinking in a Creative Environment

Allison Boyd

Imagine that you're a senior in high school, visiting colleges in the hopes of finding somewhere you can commit to for four years. While walking through the campus of a prestigious liberal arts college, you see a man in his early forties, sporting a green Mohawk, gauged ears, and Chucks. A member of a rock band, you assume. You wouldn't have given him a second thought, but your student guide smiles and waves at him, then turns to you and says, "That's Dr. Smith, the Geology professor."

Surprised? Maybe you shouldn't be. Times are changing. Where America was once thriving from industry and the assembly line, with the traditional husband-wife-2.5-kids-and-a-dog family, today the economy, business, and technology have been infiltrated by creativity. A new group of professionals has evolved: the **Creative Class.** Richard Florida, the leading expert on the Creative Class, patented the concept in 2002 and has conducted the most supporting investigations. Subsequent researchers have focused on specifics rather than the general ideas, but an overview of the broader theory is a good starting point.

The Creative Class is accurately named because this group constantly uses creative thinking in their lifestyles and careers (Bille). As a whole, the Creative Class "values creativity, individuality, differences, and merit" (Florida, *Washington Monthly*, para. 7). These values fit well with their chosen occupations, which tend to be in technology, journalism, arts, finance, entertainment, science, health care, social sciences, engineering, law, and education. These areas all involve creating new ideas, theories, or products (Florida, *Washington Monthly*; Florida, Mellander & Stolarick).

The Creative Class can be divided into creative professionals and the super-creative core. **Creative professionals** work in sectors grounded in knowledge, like legal and financial fields, and they work with high-technology. They utilize information acquired through their education, which tends to be above average, in order to find or invent solutions and answers. Creativity and innovation help them to critically deliberate options, mold traditional methods to their particular need, and make independent decisions. The **super creative core,** on the other hand, goes a step beyond the creative professionals. Their professions allow them to really use creativity and craft new elements, such as in novel-writing, architecture, acting, science, think tanks, and teaching as college professors (Florida, *Washington Monthly*). They also spend their leisure time doing creative activities, such as reading, painting, singing, composing music, and writing (Bille).

Because the Creative Class can use creativity to produce an economically-useful, innovative product, this group is becoming increasingly important to the business community (Florida, "Cities"). The presence of the Creative Class in a region is highly correlated (causation is debated) with the growth, development, and prosperity of that region (Florida, *Washington Monthly*; Florida et al, "Inside") by virtue of their innovative abilities. Richard Florida has conducted extensive research and found this correlation to be true time and time again (Florida, "Cities").

These beneficial aspects of the Creative Class also positively affect cities, and so they have begun trying to attract creatives. Florida identifies three prerequisites for luring the Creative Class, which he calls the 3Ts of Economic Development:

- **Talent**—typically defined in terms of education, measured as holding at least a Bachelor's degree, but can also include measurements of innovation, based on patents per capita.

- **Technology**—concentration of high-tech industry, such as companies focused in the medical and engineering field (Florida, *Rise*).

- **Tolerance**—not only tolerance of both people and thoughts, but incorporation into the community (Florida, "Cities"). The presence of gay people, a variety of races and ethnicities, immigrants and "bohemians" (artists) is a good indicator of the level of tolerance in a community. It is assumed that if a community is tolerant of these groups, which are frequently shunned, it is also tolerant of diverse ideas. This tolerance is important to the Creative Class, as creative people often feel atypical and seek locations that welcome them regardless of their non-traditional ways of thinking and living, and allow them to express themselves without judgment (Florida, Stolarick, Gates & Knudson). They also seek an assortment of encounters that grant new and different experiences with music, art, and entertainment, accompanied by discussions with people who think differently than they do (Florida, *Washington Monthly*). Tolerance also allows them to take risks, which they often do since they are typically young, single, and childless (Florida et al, "University").

Together, these three factors create an environment favored by the Creative Class.

So what can colleges do to attract the future members of the Creative Class? The same things that cities do. The Creative Class favors certain aspects of a community:

- **Street-level culture and lifestyle amenities**—The Creative Class enjoys having a variety of options when it comes to restaurants, live music, places to interact, cafes, and night life, and will continue to hold these preferences throughout their lifetime (Bille; Florida et al, "Inside").

- **Low entry barriers**—The Creative Class highly values low entry barriers, as a result of tolerance, which allows a more extensive and diverse range of talent in business and in the community (Florida et al, "University").

- **Participatory recreation**—The Creative Class believes that entertainment should be active and prefers a hazy distinction between those who are acting and those who are observing. They dislike passive entertainment, such as watching movies, and prefer street musicians and artists (Bille; Florida, *Washington Monthly*).

- **Active sports and outdoor amenities**—The Creative Class plays sports like biking and snowboarding, not only for the physical challenge, but because offering such activities is another indication that the community welcomes and tries to oblige those who incorporate creativity and activeness into their routines. They show little interest in watching professional sports (Florida, *Washington Monthly*).

- **Authenticity**—The Creative Class seeks experience unique to the particular community and prefers historical buildings, non-mainstream music, and experiencing the local culture. They don't want a generic night of dinner at Bob Evans and a movie (Bille).

- **Universities**—Universities are a nucleus for arts, science, and education and are also natural employers of many Creative Class members, so their existence provides an advantage to attracting the Creative Class (Florida et al, "Inside").

- **People climate**—The community must recognize that people are valuable and entice them to settle by adding investments like bike trails, which have enduring value to the whole community, rather than trying to attract corporations with short-term, possibly ineffective, efforts (Florida, *Rise*).

- **Individuality**—The Creative Class dislikes conformity and seeks to express individuality through creative channels like writing, dancing, composing music and songs, and enjoy experiencing the creative efforts of others (Florida, *Rise*).

- **Meritocracy**—This concept does not refer to monetary values. Rather, the Creative Class values hard work and determination to reach their goals and appreciates respect based on accomplishments.

Companies also cater to the Creative Class with creativity-fostering accommodations, such as:

- Relaxed dress codes,

- Flexibility in terms of schedules and work hours,

- Informal recruiting techniques (Florida, *Washington Monthly*).

These aspects can be easily implemented on a college campus. To begin with, universities are appealing to creative persons because they tend to integrate the 3Ts into every aspect (Florida, "Cities"; Florida et al, "University"). They are home to the latest and most advanced technologies, which the professors and students use to create new innovations. The professors themselves are already part of the Creative Class and are some of the most knowledgeable, creative, innovative, accomplished, and diverse members of society. Students are also highly talented and work to hone their abilities, skills, and thinking processes at universities. The collaboration between these two groups produces an extraordinary amount of knowledge and talent (Florida, *Washington Monthly*), as a result of their diverse demographics. The exchange of diverse ideas, viewpoints, and experiences enriches students' and faculty members' knowledge and incites them to think outside of their natural world (Florida et al, "University"). In addition, rewards are based on merit, which the Creative Class appreciates (Florida, *Washington Monthly*).

College campuses appeal to the Creative Class for a variety of other reasons rooted in incorporating tolerance. For example, 'everyone knows' that high school is a place of cliques and ostracism and that college is that bright future where everyone can find a place to fit in based on their varying interests (i.e., low barriers to social groups). They are also ideal because they can easily offer the diverse experiences craved by the Creative Class. Where better to have a multicultural food fair than a college campus, where there are already students of many nationalities and cultures and likely to be a culinary concentration within the curriculum? In addition, campuses make perfect small-scale creative centers: areas with elevated diversity, creativity, and technology encouraging creativity and creative people to thrive (Florida, "Cities"). Also, when you think about it, what made you choose your current college? Was it really the science department's high-powered microscope or the Nobel Prize winning faculty? More than likely it was the place itself, the city surrounding it, and how welcoming the campus, the city, and the people there seemed to you. You considered the clubs and student organizations that appealed to your interests and debated if this was a place where you could explore your options and figure out who you really are as an individual. In other words, you sought a place where you could fit in, a place with the tolerance, talent, and technology.

However, not everyone is as optimistic about the existence of the Creative Class or its economic benefits. Critics attack both specifics and generalities.

Building the physical infrastructure to support the Creative lifestyle, such as bike trails, town squares, and theatres, can be costly and is frequently paid for by tax dollars. Groups such as social workers and unions, who are concerned with the interests of the working class, paint Florida's ideas as elitist and would prefer that valuable government funds be spent on badly needed social programs (Malanga).

The most common complaint is that the connection between the Creative Class and the economic benefits touted by Florida is correlational, not causational. It is very possible that social, intellectual, and human capitals, which are part of the Creative Class, are more responsible for economic growth and development than the more broadly-defined Creative Class. In addition, the Creative Class may be a product of economic growth, not an initiator. Even worse, there is a chicken-and-egg problem: creative, diverse and economically fit cities attract the creative class, who make the city creative, diverse and economically fit (Hoyman).

Despite the criticism, cities across the nation have happily accepted Florida's Creative Class and Creative Cities. Universities could also consider the theory and apply it, as they are not faced with many of the obstacles with which the public sector contends. However, it should also be noted that universities by themselves cannot generate a creative city, as Florida discusses in his book, *The Rise of the Creative Class*. They need the support of their community to help establish and broaden the technology, tolerance, talent, and lifestyle amenities required by the Creative Class. Regardless, within themselves universities can be mini-creative centers and possess the ability to attract college students who will one day be active and influential members of the Creative Class, and thus of the business world, the economy, and the nation (Florida, *Rise*).

Creative Concepts

- The **Creative Class** focuses on using creativity to foster economic development, which is beneficial to communities, businesses, and the general population.

- To attract the Creative Class, cities must have **tolerance**, **talent**, and **technology**.

- College campuses are natural mini-creative centers and can be formulated to attract future members of the Creative Class through a variety of methods.

Exercises

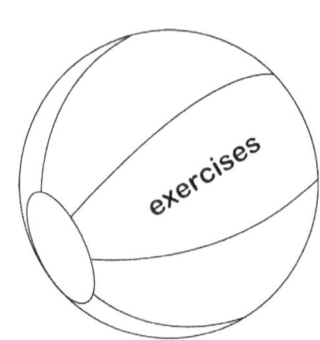

1. Divide the class into several groups. Before getting into a discussion or lecture about the Creative Class, ask them to remember what attracted them to the college. What aspects did they consider? What influenced their decision? See how the responses align with the preferences of the Creative Class.

2. Divide the class into several groups. After discussing what cities and universities can do to attract the Creative Class, instruct the students to begin observing their own campus, with these questions in mind: What aspects of this campus and this particular college life conform to the ideals of the Creative Class? What could be changed to attract the Creative Class? Are there aspects that might drive the Creative Class away? Discuss and compare the observations during the next class.

3. Set up a debate where students are encouraged to argue both sides of the Creative Class issue.

References

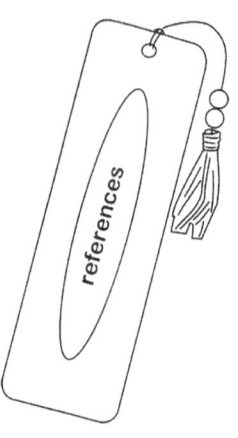

Bille, Trine. "Cool, Funky, and Creative? The Creative Class and Preferences for Leisure and Culture." *International Journal of Cultural Policy* 16.4 (2010): 466-96. *EBSCOhost*. Web. 14 Oct. 2011.

Florida, Richard. *The Rise of the Creative* Class. New York: Basic Books, 2002. Print.

---. "The Rise of the Creative Class." *Washington Monthly*, May 2002. Web. 10 Oct. 2011.

---. "Cities and the Creative Class." *City & Community* 2.1 (2003): 3-19. *EBSCOhost*. Web. 19 Oct. 2011.

Florida, Richard, Charlotta Mellander, and Kevin Stolarik. "Inside the Black Box of Regional Development—Human Capital, the Creative Class and Tolerance." *Journal of Economic Growth* 8.5 (2008): 615-49. *Google Scholar*. Web. 20 Oct. 2011.

Florida, Richard, Gary Gates, Brian Knudson, and Brian Stolarick. "The University and the Creative Economy." www.creativeclass.com. December 2006. *Google Scholar*. Web. 20 Oct. 2011.

Hoyman, Michele, and Christopher Faricy. "It Takes a Village: A Test of the Creative Class, Social Capital, and Human Capital Theories." *Urban Affairs Review* 44.3 (2009): 311-33. *EBSCOhost*. Web. 20 Oct. 2011.

Malanga, Steven. "The Curse of the Creative Class." *City Journal*, 2004. Web. 20 Oct. 2011.

Afterword

Convinced? Have the previous pages persuaded you how important Applied Creative Thinking is and how it can be used to help you take control of your future? If so and you want to improve that thinking, here are some practical tips.

Exercise regularly. According to developmental molecular biologist John Medina, "Exercise boosts brain power" and "the gold standard appears to be aerobic exercise, 30 minutes at a clip, two or three times a week. Add a strengthening regimen and you get even more cognitive benefit" (15). And if you try creative thinking shortly after this vigorous exercise (unless you're exhausted), the creativity has a greater potential for effectiveness.

- Develop a creative environment.

- Actively participate in one creative activity each week.

- Read books and articles about creative persons (and, no, the *National Inquirer* doesn't count).

- Write something creative, be it fiction or non-, for at least five minutes/day.

- Associate with a variety of people. Develop acquaintances with people from other cultures, backgrounds, and interests.

- Take risks (within reason); be willing to fail.

References

Medina, John. *Brain Rules*. Seattle: Pear Press, 2008. Print.

Appendix

Creativity Articles for Further Reading

Allison Boyd

In the process of writing this book, we conducted extensive research on creativity, innovation, and methods of teaching. Unfortunately, we were unable to actually use it all. However, the information we found is excellent and should not be ignored. What follows is a list of recommended reading. These articles will further help you understand creativity and how to encourage it in your life (some URLs are included to help you).

Agin, Erika and Tracy Gibson. "Developing an Innovative Culture." *T+D* 64.7 (2010): 52-55. *EBSCOhost.* Web. 12 Oct. 2011.

Berrett, Dan. "Which Core Matters More?" *The Chronicle of Higher Education* 58.6 (2011): A11-13. *EBSCOhost.* Web. 13 Oct. 2011.

Bille, Trine. "Cool, Funky and Creative? The Creative Class and Preferences for Leisure and Culture." *International Journal of Cultural Policy* 16.4 (2010): 466-96. *EBSCOhost.* Web. 13 Oct. 2011

Bilton, Chris. "Manageable Creativity." *International Journal of Cultural Policy* 16.3 (2010): 255-69. *EBSCOhost.* Web. 20 Oct. 2011.

Bono, Milo. "How to Generate Original Creative Ideas With Random Word Stimulation." *Innovation Tools.* 9 Aug. 2009. Web. 9 Sept. 2009. <http://www.innovationtools.com/Articles/ArticleDetails.asp?a=453>.

Bronson, Po and Ashley Merryman. "The Creativity Crisis." *Newsweek* 10 July 2010. Web. 29 Dec. 2010. <http://www.newsweek.com/2010/07/10/the-creativity-crisis.print.html>.

Bronson, Po and Ashley Merryman. "Forget Brainstorming." *Newsweek* 12 July 2010. Web. 29 Dec. 2010. <http://www.newsweek.com/2010/07/12/forget-brainstorming.print.html>.

Caridad Garcia-Cepero, Maria. "The Enrichment Triad Model: Nurturing Creative-Productivity Among College Students." *Innovations in Education & Teaching International* 45.3 (2008): 295-302. *EBSCOhost.* Web. 18 Oct. 2011.

"Concept to Classroom: Tapping into Multiple Intelligences." Thirteen, 2004. Web. 28 Sept. 2011. < http://www.thirteen.org/edonline/concept2class/mi/index.html>.

Cowen, John. "Embrace Constraints: How Limiting Yourself Won't Limit Your Designs." Onextrapixel. 20 Aug. 2010. Web. 1 Sept. 2011. <http://www.onextrapixel.com/2010/08/30/embrace-constraints-how-limiting-yourself-wont-limit-your-designs/>.

"Creativity Strategies from the 2010 CPE Dinner." *Noel Studio for Academic Creativity*. 6 Jul. 2010. Web. 18 Oct. 2011. <http://www.studio.eku.edu/creativitystrategiescpe2010.php>.

Cropley, David and Arthur Cropley. "Recognizing and Fostering Creativity in Technological Design Education." *International Journal of Design Education* 20.3 (2010): 345-58. *EBSCOhost*. Web. 14 Oct. 2011.

De Miranda, Paulo, Jose Alberto Aranha and Julia Zardo. "Creativity: People, Environment and Culture, the Key Elements in Its Understanding and Interpretation." *Science & Public Policy* 36.7 (2009): 523-35. *EBSCOhost*. Web. 20 Oct. 2011.

Demirkan, Halim, and Deniz Hasirci. "Hidden Dimensions of Creativity Elements in Design Process." *Creativity Research Journal* 21.2/3 (2009): 294-301. *EBSCOhost*. Web. 12 Oct. 2011.

Eby, Douglas. "Creativity and Flow Psychology." *Talent Development Resources*. Web. 19 Oct. 2011. <http://talentdevelop.com/articles/Page8.html>.

Fielder, Dan. "Activities for Creative Thinking in Science." *EHow.com*. 22 Feb. 2011. Web. 12 Oct. 2011. <http://www.ehow.com/info_7960375_Activities-creative-thinking-science.html>.

Florida, Richard. "The Rise of the Creative Class." *The Washington Monthly*. May 2002. Web. 8 Sept. 2011. <http://www.washingtonmonthly.com/features/2001/0205.florida.html>.

Gibbs, Nancy. "Eureka!" *Time* 22 Nov. 2010: 112. Print.

Gibson, Robyn. "Points of Departure." *Teaching in Higher Education* 15.5 (2010): 607-13. Print.

Golubtchik, Benna. "The Multiple Intelligences Classroom: Matching Teaching Methods With How Students Learn." *The New Teachers Handbook*. Ed. Martha Upton. *Teachersnetwork.org*. Web. 28 Sept. 2011. <http://www.thirteen.org/edonline/concept2class/mi/index.html>.

Gross, Mark and Ellen Yi-Kuen Do. "Educating the New Makers: Cross-Disciplinary Creativity." *Leonardo* 42.3 (2009): 210-15. *EBSCOhost*. Web. 14 Oct. 2011.

Gruenfeld, Elizabeth. "Thinking Creatively is Thinking Critically." *New Directions for Youth Development* 2010.125 (2010): 71-83. *EBSCOhost*. Web. 12 Oct. 2011.

Hardiman, Mariale M. "The Creative-Artistic Brain." *Mind, Brain, and Education: Neuroscience Implications for the Classroom*. Ed. David Sousa. Bloomington, IN: Solution Tree, 2010. 227-46. Print.

Harding, Taloe. "Fostering Creativity for Leadership and Leading Change." *Arts Education Policy Review* 111.2 (2010): 51-53. *EBSCOhost*. Web. 20 Oct. 2011..

Harrison, Sam. "Be Inspired to Innovate." *Communications World* 26.1 (2009): 16-20. *EBSCOhost*. Web. 28 Sept. 2011.

Heathfield, Susan. "Creative Thinking Matters." *About.com*. Web. 27 Sept. 2011. <http://humanresources.about.com/od/motivationsucces3/a/learn_read.htm>.

Hope, Samuel. "Creativity, Content, and Policy." *Arts Education Policy Review* 111.2 (2010): 39-47. *EBSCOhost.* Web. 12 Oct. 2011..

Huber, Marsha. "Shoeboxes and Taxes: Integrated Course Design Unleashes New Creativity for a Veteran Teacher." *New Directions for Teaching & Learning* 2009.119 (Fall2009): 9-15. *EBSCOhost.* Web. 12 Oct. 2011.

Hunter, Dan and Dan Bosley."Creative Thinking in the Classroom." *The Boston Globe.* 23 Feb. 2008. Web. 17 Sept. 2011. < http://www.boston.com/bostonglobe/editorial_opinion/oped/articles/2008/02/23/creative_thinking_in_the_classroom/>.

Jin, Yan and Oren Benami. "Creative Patterns and Stimulation in Conceptual Design." *Artificial Intelligence for Engineering Design, Analysis and Manufacturing* 24.2 (2010): 191-209. *EBSCOhost.* Web. 20 Oct. 2011.

Johnson, Steve. "The Genius of the Tinkerer." *The Wall Street Journal* [New York City] 25-26 Sept. 2010. Review sec: C1-C2. Print.

Klieman, Paul. "Towards Transformation: Conceptions of Creativity in Higher Education." *Innovations in Education & Teaching International.* 45.3 (2008): 209-17. *EBSCOhost.* Web. 12 Oct. 2011.

Krauss-Whitbourne, Susan. "Creativity and Successful Brain Aging: Going with the Flow." *Psychology Today.* 23 Mar. 2010. Web. 3 Oct. 2011. < http://www.psychologytoday.com/collections/201109/do-you-go-the-flow/creativity-and-successful-brain-aging-going-the-flow>.

Kudryavtsev, Vladimir. "The Phenomenon of Child Creativity." *International Journal of Early Years Education* 19.1 (2011): 45-53. *EBSCOhost.* Web. 12 Oct. 2011.

Lencioni, Pat. "How to Spark Innovation and Craetivity." *Businessweek* 13 Oct. 2009. Web. 12 Sept. 2011. <http://www.businessweek.com/managing/content/oct2009/ca20091013_224181.htm>.

Leitham, Keith. "Exploring our Complex Math Identities." *Mathematics Teaching in the Middle School* 16.4 (2010): 224-31. *EBSCOhost.* Web. 12 Oct. 2011.

Lehrer, Jonah. "Building a Thinking Room." *The Wall Street Journal* [New York City] 30 Apr.-1 May 2011: C12. Print.

Liberman, Nira and Oren Shapira. "Does Falling in Love Make Us More Creative?" *Scientific American* 29 Sept. 2009. Web. 12 Oct. 2011. <http://www.scientificamerican.com/article.cfm?id=does-falling-in-love-make>.

Litchfield, Robert, Jinyan Fan, and Vincent Brown. "Directing Idea Generation Using Brainstorming with Specific Novelty Goals." *Motivation & Emotion* 35.2 (2011): 135-43. *EBSCOhost.* Web. 12 Oct. 2011.

Livingston, Larry. "Teaching Creativity in Higher Education." *Arts Education Policy Review* 111.2 (2010): 59-62. *EBSCOhost.* Web. 12 Oct. 2011.

Long-Lingo, Elizabeth and Steven J. Tepper. "The Creative Campus: Time for a 'C' Change." *The Chronicle of Higher Education* [Washington, D.C.] 10 Oct. 2010: A28-A29. Print.

McGuigan, Jim. "Doing a Florida Thing: The Creative Class Thesis and Cultural Policy." *International Journal of Cultural Policy* 15.3 (2009): 291-300. *EBSCOhost.* Web. 14 Oct. 2011.

McKay, Brett and Kate McKay. "The Secret of Great Men: Deliberate Practice." *The Art of Manliness* 7 Nov. 2010. Web. 28 Sept. 2011. <http://artofmanliness.com/2010/11/7/the-secret-of-great-men-deliberate-practice/>.

McKethan, Robert, Erik Rabinowitz, and Michael Kernodle. "Multiple Intelligences in Virtual and Traditional Skill Instructional Learning Environments." *Physical Educator* 67.3 (2010): 156-68. *EBSCOhost*. Web. 12 Oct. 2011.

McWilliam, Erica. "From School to Café and Back Again: Responding to the Learning Demands of the Twenty-First Century." *International Journal of Leadership in Education* 14.3 (2011): 257-68. *EBSCOhost*. Web. 14 Oct. 2011.

O'Banion, Terry, Laura Weidnew, and Cynthia Wilson. "Creating a Culture of Innovation in the Community College." *Community College Journal of Research & Practice* 35.6 (2011): 470-83. *EBSCOhost*. Web. 12 Oct. 2011.

Paulus, Paul, Daniel Levine, Vincent Brown, Ali Minai, and Simona Doboli. "Modeling Ideational Creativity in Groups: Connecting Cognitive, Neural, and Computational Approaches." *Small Group Research* 41.6 (2010): 688-724. *EBSCOhost*. Web. 20 Oct. 2011.

Peter D. Hart Research Associates, Inc. "How Should Colleges Prepare Students to Succeed in Today's Global Economy?" Rep. Association of American Colleges and Universities, 28 Dec. 2006. Web. 20 Oct. 2011. <http://www.aacu.org/advocacy/leap/documents/Re8097abcombined.pdf>.

"Play, Creativity, and Learning: Why Play Matters for Kids and Adults." *Helpguide.org*. Web. 3 Oct. 2011. <http:www.helpguide.org/life/creative_play_fun_games.htm>.

Rinkevich, Jennifer. "Creative Teaching: Why it Matters and Where to Begin." *Clearing House* 84.5 (2011): 219-23. *EBSCOhost*. Web. 12 Oct. 2011.

Richtel, Matt. "Digital Devices Deprive Brain of Needed Downtime." *The New York Times* 24 Aug. 2010. Web. 25 Aug. 2010. <http://www.nytimes.com/2010/08/25/technology/25brain.html>.

Sarkar, Prabir and Amaresh Chakrabarti. "Assessing Design Creativity." *Design Studies* 32.4 (2011): 348-83. *EBSCOhost*. Web. 12 Oct. 2011.

Schmidt, Adele L. "The Battle for Creativity: Frontiers in Science and Science Education." *BioEssays* 32.12 (2010): 1016-19. *EBSCOhost*. Web. 20 Oct. 2011.

Shellenbarger, Sue. "Better Ideas Through Failure." *The Wall Street Journal* 27 Sept. 2011. Web. 28 Sept. 2011. <http://online.wsj.com/article/SB10001424052970204010604576594671572584158.html>.

Smith-Taylor, Summer. "Effects of Studio Space on Teaching and Learning: Preliminary Findings from Two Case Studies." *Innovative Higher Education* 33.4 (2009): 217-28. *EBSCOhost*. Web. 14 Oct. 2011.

Sternberg, Robert. "Teach Creativity, Not Memorization." *The Chronicle of Higher Education* [Washington, D.C.] 10 Oct. 2010: A29. Print.

Sternberg, Robert. "What is the Common Thread of Creativity?" *American Psychologist* 56.4 (2001): 360-62. *EBSCOhost*. Web. 12 Oct. 2011.

Thomas, Kerry. "What is the Relationship Between Social Tact in Teacher-Pupil Exchanges and Creativity? Reconceptualising Functional Causes of Creativity in Artmaking." *International Journal of Art & Design Education*, 29.2 (2010): 134-42. *EBSCOhost*. Web. 12 Oct. 2011.

Treffinger, Donald. "Myth 5: Creativity is Too Difficult to Measure." *Gifted Child Quarterly* 53.4 (2009): 245-47. *EBSCOhost*. Web. 20 Oct. 2011.

Warner, Scott and Kerri Myers. "The Creative Classroom: The Role of Space and Place Toward Facilitating Creativity." *Technology Teacher* 69.4 (2009/2010): 28-34. *EBSCOhost*. Web. 12 Oct. 2011.

Waters, Douglas. "Understanding Strategic Thinking and Developing Strategic Thinkers." *Joint Forces Quarterly* 63.4 (2011): 113-119. Print.

Watkins, Diane. "Multiple Intelligences Learning Style." *EHow.com*. Web. 29 Sept. 2011. <http://www.ehow.com/facts_5200817_multiple-intelligences-learning-style.html>.

Wright, Steve. " 'In the Zone': Enjoyment, Creativity, and the Nine Elements of Flow." *MeaningandHappiness.com* 5 Sept. 2008. Web. 3. Oct. 2011. http://www.meaningand-happiness.com/zone-enjoyment-creativity-elements-flow/26/.

Yilmaz, S., C.M. Seifert, and R. Gonzales. "Cognitive Heuristics in Design: Instructional Strategies to Increase Creativity in Idea Generation." *Artificial Intelligence for Engineering Design, Analysis and Manufacturing* 24.3 (2010): 335-55. *EBSCOhost*. Web. 14 Oct. 2011.

Zagorski, Nick. "Fostering Creativity in Science." *ASMBMtoday* June 2011. Web. 12 Oct. 2011. <http://www.asmbm.org/asbmbtday/asbmbtoday_article.aspx?id=13069&page_id=1>.

Appendix
Definitions of Creativity

Allison Boyd

Everyone has a different opinion of "creativity," and hopefully you are now able to form your own. While writing this book, we came across various definitions of creativity and related quotes which seemed to capture elements of creativity, whether it was the process of developing creativeness, the courage to be creative, the creative end result, or the sheer enjoyment derived from the creative mind. They come from all sorts of sources—Disney animators, business entrepreneurs, CEOs, politicians, creativity experts, geniuses, teachers, writers, poets, philosophers, psychologists, and musicians—demonstrating that creativity and innovation are present in every walk of life. We present them to you here.

"Each moment of our life, we either invoke or destroy our dreams." *–Stuart Wilde*

"Daring ideas are like chessmen moved forward; they may be beaten, but they may start a winning game." *–Goethe*

"People who don't take risks generally make about 2 big mistakes a year, people who do take risks generally make about 2 big mistakes a year" *–Peter Drucker*

"Curiosity about life in all of its aspects, I think, is still the secret of great creative people." *–Leo Burnett*

"A life spent making mistakes is not only more honorable, but more useful than a life spent doing nothing." *–George Bernard Shaw*

"To avoid criticism say nothing, do nothing, be nothing." *–Aristotle*

"The things we fear most in organizations—fluctuations, disturbances, imbalances—are the primary sources of creativity." *—Margaret J. Wheatley*

"Creativity is thinking up new things. Innovation is doing new things."
–*Theodore Levitt*

"It is better to have enough ideas for some of them to be wrong, than to be always right by having no ideas at all." –*Edward de Bono*

"The creative person wants to be a know-it-all. He wants to know about all kinds of things-ancient history, nineteenth century mathematics, current manufacturing techniques, hog futures. Because he never knows when these ideas might come together to form a new idea. It may happen six minutes later, or six months, or six years. But he has faith that it will happen."
—*Carl Ally*

"You can't wait for inspiration, you have to go after it with a club." –*Jack London*

"Listen to anyone with an original idea, no matter how absurd it may sound at first. If you put fences around people, you get sheep. Give people the room they need." —*William McKnight*

"Everyone who's ever taken a shower has had an idea. It's the person who gets out of the shower, dries off and does something about it who makes a difference." —*Nolan Bushnell*

"Because of their courage, their lack of fear, they (creative people) are willing to make silly mistakes. The truly creative person is one who can think crazy; such a person knows full well that many of his great ideas will prove to be worthless. The creative person is flexible; he is able to change as the situation changes, to break habits, to face indecision and changes in conditions without undue stress. He is not threatened by the unexpected as rigid, inflexible people are." —*Frank Goble*

"Invention strictly speaking, is little more than a new combination of those images which have been previously gathered and deposited in the memory; nothing can come from nothing." —*Sir Joshua Reynolds*

"Creativity is contagious. Pass it on." —*Albert Einstein*

"The principle goal of education is to create men who are capable of doing new things, not simply of repeating what other generations have done – men who are creative, inventive and discoverers." —*Jean Piaget*

"An idea that is developed and put into action is more important than an idea that exists only as an idea." —*Edward de Bono*

"To live a creative life, we must lose our fear of being wrong." —*Joseph Chilton Pierce*

"You can't use up creativity. The more you use, the more you have."
—*Maya Angelou*

"Do not fear to be eccentric in opinion, for every opinion now accepted was once eccentric." —*Bertrand Russell*

"Life is trying things to see if they work." –*Ray Bradbury*

"There is no doubt that creativity is the most important human resource of all. Without creativity, there would be no progress, and we would be forever repeating the same patterns." –*Edward de Bono*

"To raise new questions, new possibilities, to regard old problems from a new angle requires a creative imagination and marks the real advance in science." –*Albert Einstein*

"The greatest danger for most of us is not that our aim is too high and we miss it, but that it is too low and we reach it." –*Michelangelo*

"The difference between the people at the top of the ladder and those at… the bottom is so basic. The people at the top have learned how to handle good ideas, but those who stay in the middle or the bottom… have never learned to catch, harbor and handle creative thoughts." –*Robert H. Schuller*

"Today more than ever, we must cultivate the creative and innovative potential of every employee in the organization. Everyone in the organization must be capable of thinking creatively and be willing to try new approaches which transcend their own roles, departments and processes." –*Andrew Papageorge*

"Connections are the wellspring of creative thought, and the more consciously you practice opening your mind to make connections, the better you will be at making them and the more you will make them." –*Jeff Mauzy and Richard Harriman*

"Creative thinking is not a talent, it is a skill that can be learnt. It empowers people by adding strength to their natural abilities which improves teamwork, productivity and where appropriate profits." –*Edward de Bono*

"Just encouraging innovation is not enough. You need to initiate programs that show people how they can use creative techniques to come up with new solutions. People need training in order to learn the skills to develop the confidence to try new methods." –*Paul Sloane*

"One of the great problems with our education system is that it teaches that for almost every question there is one correct answer. Unfortunately the real world is not like that. For almost every problem there are multiple solutions. We have to unlearn the school approach and instead adopt an attitude of always looking for more and better answers." –*Paul Sloane*

"To survive and prosper in the long-term, people in companies need to create and innovate. And they need to do so as regularly and reliably as they breathe." –*Jeff and Richard Harriman*

"The world leaders in innovation and creativity will also be world leaders in everything else." –*Harold R. McAlidon*

"Like a highly intelligent child with a pail of Legos, a genius is constantly combining and recombining ideas, images, and thoughts into different combinations in their conscious and subconscious minds." –*Michael Michalko*

"Creative geniuses are geniuses because they know 'how' to think instead of 'what' to think." —*Michael Michalko*

"While magic sometimes happens in one mind alone, it most often occurs as sparks fly between minds." –*Joyce Wycoff*

"There is no creativity in certainty; no discovery in absolutes; no breakthrough ideas birthed in the bright light of established fact." —*Joyce Wycoff*

"We grew up on the 3 R's: reading, writing and 'rithmetic... But today we need more. Today's basic 3 I's are intuition, inspiration and innovation." –*Grace McGartland*

"Many ideas grow better when transplanted into another mind than in the one where they sprung up." –*Oliver Wendell Holmes*

"Most of my ideas belonged to other people who never bothered to develop them." –*Thomas Edison*

"Ideas are not abstractions but experiences. They must be carried alive into the heart." –*John Clayton*

"Instead of pouring knowledge into people's heads, we need to help them grind a new set of eyeglasses so that we can see the world in a new way." –*J.S. Brown*

"Innovation distinguishes between a leader and a follower." –*Steve Jobs*

"Problems cannot be solved by the same level of thinking that created them." –*Albert Einstein*

"Imagination is the beginning of creation. You imagine what you desire, you will what you imagine, and at last you create what you will." –*George Bernard Shaw*

"Creativity is allowing yourself to make mistakes. Art is knowing which ones to keep." –*Scott Adams*

"Sometimes when you innovate, you make mistakes. It is best to admit them quickly, and get on with improving your other innovations." –*Steve Jobs*

"Creativity comes from trust. Trust your instincts. And never hope more than you work." –*Rita Mae Brown*

"Don't think. Thinking is the enemy of creativity. It's self-conscious, and anything self-conscious is lousy. You can't try to do things. You simply must do things." –*Ray Bradbury*

"Creativity is a lot like looking at the world through a kaleidoscope. You look at a set of elements, the same ones everyone else sees, but then reassemble those floating bits and pieces into an enticing new possibility. Effective leaders are able to." –*Rosabeth Moss Kanter*

"Creativity in inventing, experimenting, growing, taking risks, breaking rules, making mistakes, and having fun." –*Mary Lou Cook*

"Creativity can solve almost any problem. The creative act, the defeat of habit by originality overcomes everything." –*George Lois*

"Conditions for creativity are to be puzzled; to concentrate; to accept conflict and tension; to be born everyday; to feel a sense of self." –*Eric Fromm*

"Creativity involves breaking out of established patterns in order to look at things in a different way." –Edward de Bon

"Necessity is the mother of invention, it is true, but its father is creativity, and knowledge is the midwife." –Jonathan Schattke

"Uncertainty and mystery are energies of life. Don't let them scare you unduly, for they keep boredom at bay and spark creativity." –*R.I. Fitzhenry*

"The creation of something new is not accomplished by the intellect but by the play instinct acting from inner necessity. The creative mind plays with the object it loves." –*Carl Jung*

"Observe everything. Communicate well. Draw, draw, draw." –*Frank Thomas*

"To live a creative life, we must lose our fear of being wrong." –*Joseph Chilton Pearce*

"Creativity represents a miraculous coming together of the uninhibited energy of the child with its apparent opposite and enemy, the sense of order imposed on the disciplined adult intelligence." –*Normal Podhoretz*

"Creative work is play. It is free speculation using materials of one's chosen form." –*Stephen Nachmanovitch*

"We do not need magic to transform our world. We carry all the power we need inside ourselves already. We have the power to imagine better." –*J. K. Rowling*

"Creativity is not the finding of a thing, but the making something out of it after it is found." –*James Russell Lowell*

"This is patently absurd; but whoever wishes to become a philosopher must learn not to be frightened by absurdities." –*Bertrand Russell*

"I think a hero is an ordinary individual who finds strength to preserve and endure in spite of overwhelming obstacles." –*Christopher Reeve*

"There are two ways of being creative. One can sing and dance. Or one can create an environment in which singers and dancers flourish." –*Warren G. Bennis*

"Judge a man by his questions rather than his answers." –*Voltaire*

"Properly practiced creativity can make one ad do the work of ten." –*William Bernbach*

"Science may set limits to knowledge, but should not set limits to imagination." –*Bertrand Russell*

"Science is facts; just as houses are made of stones, so is science made of facts; but a pile of stones is not a house and a collection of facts is not necessarily science." –*Henri Poincare*

"The most exciting phrase to hear in science, the one that heralds new discoveries, is not "Eureka!" (I found it!) but 'That's funny…'" –*Isaac Asimov*

"The noun itself becomes a verb. This flashpoint of creation in the present moment is where work and play merge." –*Stephen Nachmanovitch*

"Creative thinking may mean simply the realization that there's no particular virtue in doing things the way they have always been done." –*Rudolf Flesch*

"Creativity in science could be described as the act of putting two and two together to make five." –*Arthur Koestler*

"The ideal engineer is a composite… He is not a scientist, he is not a mathematician, he is not a sociologist or a writer; but he may use the knowledge and techniques of any or all of these disciplines in solving engineering problems." –*N.W. Doughtery*

"It's hard for corporations to understand that creativity is not just about succeeding. It's about experimenting and discovering." –*Gordon Mackenzie*

"Genius is one percent inspiration, ninety-nine percent perspiration." –*Thomas Edison*

"A hunch is creativity trying to tell you something." –*Frank Capra*

"Good ideas are not adopted automatically. They must be driven into practice with courageous patience." –*Hyman Rickover*

"Do something. If it doesn't work, do something else. No idea is too crazy." –*Jim Hightower*

"I can't understand why people are so frightened of new ideas. I'm frightened of the old ones." –*John Cage*

"I am among those who think that science has great beauty. A scientist in his laboratory is not only a technician: he is also a child placed before natural phenomena which impress him like a fairy tale." –*Marie Curie*

"The important thing in science is not so much to obtain new facts as to discover new ways of thinking about them." –*Sir William Bragg*

"You are today where your thoughts have brought you; you will be tomorrow where your thoughts take you." –*James Lane Allen*

"Change your thoughts and you change your world." –Norman Vincent Peale

"Just because something doesn't do what you planned it to do doesn't mean it's useless." –*Thomas Edison*

"Results! Why, man, I have gotten a lot of results. I know several thousand things that won't work." –*Thomas Edison*

"I never teach my pupils. I only attempt to provide the conditions in which they can learn." –*Albert Einstein*

"Creativity is imaginative activity fashioned so as to produce outcomes that are both original and of value." –*National Advisory Committee on Creative & Cultural Education, 1990*

"Creativity constructs new tools and new outcomes – new embodiments of knowledge. It constructs new relationships, rules, communities of practice and new connections – new social practices." – *Peter Knight*

Appendix

Further Exercises

1. Since 1997 the number of patent applications in this country has doubled so that now half a million inventors/year apply for patents. Describe in simple terms something you would either like to patent or see patented, and then sell that something to an audience of your peers.

2. According to *The Wall Street Journal* (April 30-May 1, 2011, C12), researchers at the University of British Columbia conducted an experiment in the psychology of buildings because they were interested in how work environments influence our moods, our ideas, and even our health. Among their discoveries were that test-takers in rooms painted red were more accurate and paid more attention to detail; on the other hand, people in blue rooms were more accomplished on assignments necessitating imagination. In light of these discoveries, what color do you think classrooms should be painted?

3. Narrative theorists often dichotomize story conclusions into open endings and closed endings. Closed endings are found in movies such as *Animal House* and *Remember the Titans* wherein just before the final credits viewers are told the eventual fates of the major characters. Open endings occur in stories such as "The Open Window" and "The Lady or the Tiger?" wherein the reader is left with a sense of ambiguity, of not knowing the final fates of characters. Which type do you prefer? Do you always like your ending that way? What do you think your preference reveals about your personality?

4. In hard economic times, school boards often pare curriculums down, and among the first classes to go are arts and athletics. Reflect on your education until now. Arts and athletics are also not usually tested the way math, English, and the sciences are. Can you make a case for not only keeping these often-slashed courses, but for increasing their presence in the curriculum?

5. Do you think your diet has any effect on your creativity? Name some food/beverages that you think would be an asset. What might be detrimental?

6. At Google, engineers are instructed that one day/week they **must** spend the time working not on traditional Research and Development (R&D), but on creating something that does not fall within the parameters of their job description. Why do you think a successful company such as Google maintains such a policy?

7. The great sailor and pop culture sage Popeye claims, "I yam what I yam and tha's all that I yam." On the other hand, brain researchers use the term neuroplasticity to describe the brain's ability to change in response to experiences. Which of the following exercises do you think would support Popeye and which the brain researchers?

- Dancing Hip-hop style

- Learning to speak Old English

- Mastering finish carpentry

- Playing a ukulele

- Memorizing multiplication tables

- Building a Lego project

- Walking on stilts

- Mastering Tae Bo.

8. According to the American Management Association's 2010 Critical Skills Survey, 66% of top managers deem creativity/innovation important to advancement in their company. Do you think they assess their employees as better than average at that skill at a higher or lower rate?

9. Just when you think there's nothing left to create, someone invalidates your premise. Do you think we play all the games the world will ever know? In 2005, a group of Kentucky high school students mashed up not a new song, but a new game. Hantis is a combination of "hands" and "tennis" that uses one tennis ball, a net, and four adjacent tables. From there, the rules vary depending on the participants (you can read more about hantis at "It's a Game! It's a Sport! It's Hantis!" *Lexington Herald-Leader*, 11 October 2011: B1, B4). Your assignment, should you choose to accept, is to create another new game that combines elements of extant games; you must list the equipment needed and the basic rules.

10. In his poem "My Last Duchess," Robert Browning has his persona, the Duke of Ferrara, recount the tale of his beautiful late wife in a mere 56 lines. Tellingly, the Duke packs this short narrative with over 20 first-person pronouns, suggesting the egotism that may have led to the Duchess' death. And aren't we all a little too much like Browning's self-centered aristocrat? To test yourself, write a note to a friend **without** using I, me, my, mine, or myself.

11. Mel Brooks made a fortune with his movie *Young Frankenstein* in which he turned the horror genre on its ear by remaking the 1939 classic as a comedy. Flex your creative muscles by turning your favorite horror film, story, novel, or TV show into a comedy, or transform a favorite TV comedy into a serious drama.

12. Have you ever been driving along in your car or sitting alone in your room when a song played that took you back in time so that you experienced emotions you hadn't felt in years? Or perhaps you suddenly found a photo that gave you the warm fuzzies. The poet John Keats called this experience "negative capability." Proust experienced the same sensation by simply drinking a cup of tea. Listen to some "golden oldies" or flip through some pics from the past and record the emotions summoned up. Can you recreate the experience wherein you first had these emotions (even harder, can you describe the experience without specifically noting the emotions it engendered)?

13. Psychologists tell us that around 85% of the sensory information we obtain comes to us visually. Choose a familiar object and describe it in a paragraph using as many senses as possible—excluding sight.

14. *The Oxford English Dictionary* (OED) is one of the world's astounding publications. Where a typical desk dictionary may devote several lines to defining a word, the OED might spend a page. Choose a favorite magazine, turn to a random page, and with your eyes closed stop your finger somewhere on the page. Picking the noun or verb nearest your finger, write down every meaning for that word you know. Now use those definitions to craft individual sentences.

15. In a well-known Seinfeld episode, George decides to change his luck by doing everything the opposite of the way he typically does it. Take an hour in which you do everything (except breathing) differently from your norm. For instance, if you always eat cereal for breakfast, try eggs and toast, or if you habitually wear jeans to school, slip on a skirt (or sports coat and slacks). Does the change affect you, your attitudes, your routine, your perception of the world around you?

16. Several recent movies have involved characters who for some strange reason or another change bodies with someone totally different from them in age, culture, or race (think *Freaky Friday* or *Big*). Since you're probably not going to enter the Twilight Zone anytime soon, you can experience a change in perspective by getting to know someone different from you. Have lunch with a classmate from a different country, or volunteer to spend an afternoon at the senior center. And for a real clash, go out with someone whose political view opposes yours. Did time spent with these "others" change the way you look at life in any way?

17. In the classic TV series *Kung Fu*, the young monk (aka Grasshopper) is admonished to "touch the color of the sky." His mentor was suggesting a

type of synesthesia, or giving traits of one sense to another as in "loud pink" or "gravelly bass note." Make up your own synesthetic phrase.

18. A Victorian wit held that nothing succeeds like excess. Even though you may not be wild about Oscar, write a news bulletin in which you describe an ordinary, even pedestrian event in extraordinary terms so as to make it sensational.

19. Your friend Tom is an honest person ("Honest as the day is long," your grandfather might say), and you could describe him simply, saying, "Tom is honest." Now come up with as many ways as you can to suggest his honest without using that word.

20. The old TV character MacGyver was so famous for using ordinary objects for extraordinary purposes that we now use the eponymous verb "to MacGyver" to mean just that (though he did have a predilection for using duct tape as a solve-all). Choose any object from your room (No duct tape, please!), and come up with five ways to use it that vary from its intended purpose.

21. Stan Lee has become a wealthy man because of his ability to create superheroes. Stan Lee it! Create your own superhero with unique powers/talents—and don't forget to provide a weakness (e.g., kryptonite) that renders your superhero vulnerable.

22. Ever want to be a fly on the wall and get credit for it? Eavesdrop on a conversation or two (No illegal bugs, please!) in a classroom or eatery. Use those words to come up with an interesting opening to a story/article.

23. A characternym is a device wherein a character's name suggests something about a character, including his/her role in a work. Either create a few characternyms on your own, or find some in your favorite medium (e.g., Max Payne).

24. Have you ever watched a movie or read a story and felt disappointed at the end because you would have concluded it differently? Choose a movie, book, or TV show and rewrite the ending so as to satisfy you.

25. Superman has his Fortress of Solitude and Batman, the Batcave—places the superheroes retreat to rest, rehab, and plan strategy. If you had such a retreat, what would you name it? What would it look like? Describe your created space in terms of size, décor, technology, even color scheme.

26. Lawrence Lessig discusses the concept of remix in creative thinking. Try synching an old family video to music. How does the music change the original message? Can you change the message to say something different?

About the Authors

Russell Carpenter, Ph.D. (University of Central Florida, 2009) is the founding Director of the Noel Studio for Academic Creativity and Assistant Professor of English at Eastern Kentucky University. The Noel Studio at EKU has a nationally unique mission and vision that emphasizes collaborative and creative approaches to developing student communication through integrating written, oral (and aural), electronic, and visual modes and media. Carpenter received a Ph.D. in Texts & Technology at UCF.

Charlie Sweet, Ph.D. (Florida State University, 1970) is the Co-Director of the Teaching & Learning Center at Eastern Kentucky University. With Hal, he has collaborated on over 800 published works, including 13 books, literary criticism, educational research, and a stint as ghostwriter of the lead novella for the *Mike Shayne Mystery Magazine*.

Hal Blythe, Ph.D. (University of Louisville, 1972) is the Co-Director of the Teaching & Learning Center at Eastern Kentucky University. With Charlie, he has collaborated on over 800 published works, including 13 books (seven in New Forums' popular *It Works for Me* series), literary criticism, and educational research.

www.ingramcontent.com/pod-product-compliance
Lightning Source LLC
Chambersburg PA
CBHW081421230426
43668CB00016B/2314